FROM EAST TO WEST

Brigid Marlin was born in Washington, DC, in January 1936, the second child in a family of six. Her father was a pioneer in airport safety, and her mother a well-known writer for children.

From babyhood, Brigid wanted to paint, and she is now a well-established artist, working and teaching in England, one of her greatest pleasures being "to make people look with new eyes".

This is her first book, although she has illustrated books written by other people.

From East to West

Awakening to a Spiritual Search

BRIGID MARLIN

Collins
FOUNT PAPERBACKS

First published in Great Britain by Fount Paperbacks, London in 1989

Printed and bound in Great Britain by
William Collins Sons & Co. Ltd, Glasgow

To A.J. in love and gratitude,
and to all the pilgrims on the journey

From the unreal lead me to the real!
From darkness lead me to light!
From death lead me to immortality!

THE BRIHAD ARANAJABA
UPANISHAD

CONTENTS

ACKNOWLEDGEMENTS

I would like to thank all the people who helped me so kindly while the book was in progress; Virginia Rogers for her wonderful hospitality and inspiration, Huey Johnson, who has been a great and unselfish supporter of artists and writers, Bill Stilwell for giving his time and advice, Carol Hamilton, Shirley Berlin and Alex Benjamin for helpful criticism. My sisters Sheila and Elisabeth and my Mother for listening and advising, my sons for putting up with the mess and confusion; a special thanks to Lesley Walmsley for dealing with my dog-eared and paint-spattered manuscript; and against her wishes I insist on acknowledging my debt to Sarah Baird-Smith, without whom this book could not have been written.

I am also grateful to writers and publishers who have allowed me to quote from their works, full details of which are given in the Notes at the back of this book.

FOREWORD

Less than a week before his untimely death in 1968, Thomas Merton visited the giant Buddhas at Polonnaruwa in Sri Lanka and experienced a blinding illumination. He spoke of being jerked out of "the habitual, half-tied vision of things", of having glimpsed what he was obscurely looking for, of "having got beyond the shadow and the disguise".

Something of this kind happened to Brigid Marlin, when, by way of Carl Jung, she first began to study the spiritual writings of the East: "A world of understanding and insight was opened to me." Those treasures of the East shed new light on the Western Christianity into which she had been born, but which had remained for her, as for many of us, un-absorbed and infantile. Wisely she decided that the only hope of making her faith real lay in becoming a pilgrim in search of the Spirit. And as guides for the journey she chose not only the great Christian writers but also Carl Jung; Buddhist teachers from Tibet, Japan, Sri Lanka; gurus from India; Middle Eastern Sufi mystics; Taoists and Confucians; Jewish philosophers; and wise old American Indians. The culling of so many sources of wisdom proved richly inspiring.

Brigid Marlin is a creative artist of considerable power and perceptiveness. But her search for truth was not merely aesthetic; it arose from a deep personal anguish and a need to make sense of a world that was falling about her ears. The extracts she has chosen for this anthology are linked together by personal experience, and are the more powerful for having answered to her own need and at times to her own despair. With her we embark on a sometimes painful journey towards self-knowledge, relentlessly stripping away the false, puncturing illusions, perceiving old truths in new ways, observing "how things really are", reaching out for that healing compassion which is nothing more or less than an openness to the world as it is.

Although I have been a friend of Brigid's for some years and have been unfailingly impressed by her wide reading and deep imaginative insights, this book comes as a revelation. From now on my own attempts to get beyond "the shadow and the disguise" will be affected by what I have read here. Brigid Marlin makes us see clearly that the Christ of Christianity is alive in other faiths, universally available to all those who seek.

As Andrew Harvey wrote in *Journey To Ladakh*, "what we have been most deprived of, as Westerners brought up in a materialistic age, is the richest, most spiritual part of our own culture". What we need – and need badly – is some kind of synthesis between Western religion and the transcendental insights of the East. Brigid Marlin's book is a step in the right direction.

MARY CRAIG

1

A Journey on Different Levels

Long after I had grown up, my religion stayed at a childish level. I was a good girl; I went to church every Sunday and kept the rules. In this way I expected God to keep to the rules too. If I kept within the letter of His Church's laws, He would look after me and make sure that nothing bad would happen to me. It was not unlike the arrangement that certain shops have in New York with the Mafia.

The trouble was that God didn't keep to my rules. One day my life fell apart: I found that my eldest son was handicapped. Later he died, and my marriage ended in divorce. My shallow faith collapsed. I had to drop all my defences, and cry for help from the depth of my inner pain. And from that depth, which I had never been aware of before, God answered me.

I saw that God didn't want my grudging obedience to the rules; He wanted me! In all the difficulties that I had to undergo after that, I felt God's presence and support helping me. It seemed that there were different levels in myself. Being a "good girl" was only the first step. In order to grow it was necessary that my faith should exist on a deeper level, and for that I would have to develop a deeper understanding of myself. I realized that I knew nothing about my own inner life, and at last I wanted to know what was going on inside me.

I developed an interest in psychology and philosophy. There were psychologists and philosophers who merely stayed on the surface, but the work of Carl Jung touched me deeply. His writings led me to study the spiritual teachings of the Eastern religions, and a world of understanding and insight was opened to me. So often when I was puzzled by a question in my

Christian faith, a light would be given on it by another teaching. I grew to feel so enriched by the great treasures of Eastern spiritual thought, that I wanted to bring them to others in the Christian tradition. However, this study was to take me many years, for I had to begin at the lowest point and in the depths of despair.

My first task was to try to sort myself out. I was a bundle of conflicting desires and fears. I had thought that because I didn't know any better my mistakes were excused but Jung's words took away that notion.

> Before the bar of nature and fate, unconsciousness is never accepted as an excuse; on the contrary there are very severe penalties for it.[1]

Jung wrote that terrible inner wars were raging in the hearts of ordinary people, who were completely unaware of this conflict unless either it betrayed itself later on as a nervous breakdown, or sometimes a shock could waken people to their inner condition, which is what had happened to me. The shock of the death of my son, followed soon after by my divorce, woke me to myself. I was led to look inside, find my inner conflicts, and by seeing them, help to resolve then.

I had to become responsible to myself for myself. I had wanted to go on being God's baby, but I began to comprehend that God's compassion is not our compassion.

> God is not nice. God is no uncle.
> God is an earthquake![2]

Soon after this a friend lent me a book by Chögyam Trungpa, a Tibetan Buddhist teacher who had fled to America from Tibet, after the Chinese occupation. To my surprise, what he wrote was not difficult to understand. It was interesting and helpful because he put things in a new way. He showed me that we must not expect God to baby us. He wrote that although usually we think of compassion as kindness or warmth (what is described in Tibetan writings as "Grandmother's love") in fact, true compassion is ruthless from the point of view of the ego, because true compassion wants us to try to overcome the ego.

> The logical voice of ego advises us to be kind to other people, to be good boys and girls and lead innocent little lives. We work at our regular jobs and rent a cosy room or apartment for ourselves; we would like to continue in this way, but suddenly something happens which tears us out of our secure little nest. Either we become extremely depressed or something outrageously painful occurs. We begin to wonder why heaven has been so unkind. "Why should God punish me? I have been a good person, I have never hurt a soul." But there is something more to life than that.
>
> We have to be jarred out of our regular, repetitive and comfortable lifestyles . . . We must begin to become compassionate and wise in the fundamental sense, open and relating to the world as it is.[3]

Up to this time I had assumed that because I was a Catholic and obeyed the rules, I had a reserved seat on the bus to Heaven; forgetting that what you don't work for, you don't value. It was time for me to get out and walk. I must make my faith my own, and to do that both thought and study were needed.

As I studied I was reminded of a toy I had been given as a child, a stereoscope. It was a pair of binoculars, into the eye pieces of which a photographic scene could be fitted. The scene was photographed from two slightly different angles, and sprang into life as a three-dimensional picture when you looked through the eye-pieces.

In the same way, by adding a different viewpoint the Oriental religions supplied an extra insight into my own religion. Their reverence for that which is sacred showed their perception of the difference between higher and lower – they were aware that there actually were different levels.

I felt the lack of this awareness in the Western culture around me, where everything has become flattened out by the television screen and jumbled together, as if no one thing is more important than another. Not only on television, but also in newspapers and magazines the flattening goes on: a starving child is juxtaposed against an ad for after-dinner mints, a cathedral is used for rock concerts, Christ is described as a super-star. It seems that we have forgotten what it is to reverence anything.

What is important is not whether someone is a Protestant, a Jew, a Catholic, a Muslim or a Buddhist; but what *kind* of Protestant, Jew, Catholic, Muslim or Buddhist they are. There are many levels of faith among those professing the same religion.

When Cerno Bokar, the West African Sufi mystic, was asked how many different kinds of faith there were, he did not begin to enumerate the different religions; instead he said that faith was what was inside a man, and the depth of the faith depended on what spiritual level a man had reached, whatever the name of the religion that he belonged to. The lowest level of inner faith he called the level of stone, the second, the level of water, and the third and highest, the level of air.

Stone faith is for those who prefer the letter of the law rather than the spirit; it is as hard and precise as stone. Those at that level think in terms of boundaries; of "us" and "them". "At times it prescribes armed warfare if this is necessary to gain respect and to assure its position."

The faith of the middle level – that of water – belongs to those who have worked and faced up to the trials of the first level, which was "of the rigid law that admits no compromise. They have triumphed over their faults and have set out on the way which leads to truth."

The faith of water gives life, it is flexible, it can solidify like ice to move nearer to the people of the lowest level, or it can rise like a vapour towards men of the highest level. The adepts of this faith stand against war, and live at peace with men and the animal kingdom.

The highest faith is called the level of air. It is pure and rises above matter. "Those who reach this faith adore God in truth in the light without colour." On this highest plane the lower levels of faith "both disappear to make a place for one sole thing, the Divine Truth which flourishes in the fields of Love and Truth."[4]

At the highest level all the faiths would join together, and there could be no violence or disagreement there. I found as I studied and tried to practise my faith from something more real inside me, that I felt a fellowship with those from other faiths who were trying to do the same. It became more and more clear that we were trying to draw near to the same God; that we were all brothers and sisters.

The forces of evil in the world do not appear to be diminishing. There is a feeling among all those of any faith who wish to work for the good of mankind, that they cannot afford to be at war with each other on sectarian grounds. There is an ecumenical spirit growing, as believers are looking more at what they have in common than at what is separating them. Above all, this is a time when each person is called on to make his or personal quest of the spirit – it is to the individual that the world looks for its salvation.

The Eastern religions can teach us about finding and developing the real self, they have found this to be an exact science. The teaching comes from many sources: from the Buddhist traditions in Tibet, Japan and Ceylon, from different gurus in India, from Jewish philosophers and the Hasidic tradition, from Sufis in the Middle East, from Taoists and the followers of Confucius in China, and from the spiritual way of the American Indian, who has a special feeling for nature.

At the end of the last century, a man called Gurdjieff, a Caucasian Greek, recognized the value of the teachings of the various schools for spiritual training in the East. He and a few companions, calling themselves "Seekers of Truth", began to search and to study. The authentic flavour of what they found is apparent in the living teaching that Gurdjieff brought back, in the form of writings, sacred dances and music, in order to make it available to "seekers of truth" in the West.

Gurdjieff points out that in order to benefit from a search, one must search with the right intent; he does not minimize the difficulties, pointing out that for knowledge to be passed on it requires great labour, both for the person who teaches and for the one who receives the knowledge.

> He who wants knowledge must himself make the initial efforts to find the source of knowledge and to approach it, taking advantage of the help and indications which are given to all, but which people, as a rule, do not want to see or recognize. Knowledge cannot come to people without effort on their own part. They understand this very well in connection with ordinary knowledge, but in the case of *great knowledge*, when they admit the possibility of its existence, they find it possible to expect something different. Everyone knows very well that if, for instance, a man wants to learn Chinese, it will take several years of intense work; everyone knows that five years are needed to grasp the principles of medicine, and perhaps twice as many years for the study of painting or music.[5]

Each of us has an inner universe that corresponds to the outer. Therefore in gaining an understanding of the laws that govern one's inner world, one can understand more of the laws that govern the outer world. However, the journey towards finding another level is not easy.

> It gradually becomes clear that the study of man has no meaning unless it is placed in the context of life as a whole and of the whole world in which he lives. The study of man is inseparable from a living study of the cosmos. Thus,

obstacles never cease to arise, and this search, which at first may appear straightforward, opens up finally on to horizons of which a man could hardly have had the slightest idea when he began.[6]

I saw that remaining in the comfort of a faith undeveloped in myself, had been deadening. The only hope for me was to move on – to become a pilgrim. The journey was horizontal, across the planes of the earth through time until my death; and vertical, trying at any moment to rise up towards the level of the spirit, and ever down deeper into my own heart, to progress there in understanding.

A tree that can fill the span of a man's arms
Grows from a downy tip;
A terrace nine storeys high
Rises from hodfuls of earth;
A journey of a thousand miles
Starts from beneath one's feet.[7]

"Of these two thousand fiery mountains," Jonaid remarked, "I have crossed only one."

"You are lucky to have crossed one", said Jorairi. "Up to now I have gone only three steps."

Shebli burst into tears.

"You are fortunate, Jonaid, to have crossed one mountain", he cried. "And you are fortunate, Jorairi, to have gone three steps. Up to now I have not even seen the dust from afar."[8]

Up! Up! Only a little life is left,
the road before you is long, and you are immersed in
illusion.[9]

2

Knowledge and Understanding

For many years I used to confuse those two words, knowledge and understanding; if at school I could repeat a mathematical formula I would say that I had understood it.

But when I found that my son was handicapped, I quickly learned the difference in the two ways people approached me about him. Both sets of people knew that my son had a problem, but those with handicapped children themselves understood how I felt. They never hurt me with thoughtless remarks.

In that way I learned that mere cleverness isn't worth very much in human terms.

This is something that has been recognized by other cultures. The Africans have a saying, "White men think too much". We in the West have given too much importance to words and information. So we have quiz shows on radio and television where people are honoured for being able to hoard scraps of useless information in their heads, without asking whether they have been able to use this information to advantage to make anything of their lives, or to create anything worthwhile.

> We Westerners need dictionaries and encyclopedias to satisfy our insatiable need to know by *always bringing back the unknown to the known*. . . . we proceed from definitions. That is what we call "liking clear ideas". But by dint of accumulating definitions we end up "by knowing everything and understanding nothing ". . . the most beautiful truth – as history has shown a thousand times over – is no use at all unless it has become the innermost experience and possession of the individual. Every unequivocal, so-

> called "clear" answer always remains stuck in the head, but only very rarely does it penetrate to the heart. The needful thing is not to *know* the truth but to *experience* it. Not to have an intellectual conception of things, but to find our way to the inner, and perhaps wordless, irrational experience – that is the great problem.[1]

A Persian proverb says: "The wise man understands the fool, for he himself was once a fool; but the fool does not understand the wise man, since he never was wise."

René Daumal wrote a satire on our dependence on information. In his book *A Night of Serious Drinking*, a learned professor boasts of a wonderful school where there is no exercise or games for the pupils. Instead the importance of physical exercise is acknowledged by making the children spend one quarter of each day studying gymnastic manuals, the lives of great athletes, and handbooks on sport, so that even the most sickly child can know all about physical culture. In the same way "reforms" have been introduced in all the other subjects so that

> Thanks to cinema, the phonograph, museums and most especially to picture books, our schoolchildren take no time at all to learn everything about art without ever having to create anything, everything about science without having to think, everything about religion without having to live.[2]

When I was expecting my first child, I bought several child-care manuals. As I read them I got more and more discouraged. Bringing up a child seemed so complicated; there were so many things that could go wrong! But when I actually had the child, everything was different. Caring for the child seemed to come naturally, from a part of me that I didn't know existed.

> In the sphere of practical activity people know very well the difference between mere knowledge and understanding. They realize that to know and *to know how to do* are two different things, and that *knowing how to do* is not created

> by knowledge alone. But outside the sphere of practical activity people do not clearly understand what "understanding" means.
>
> As a rule, when people realize that they do not understand a thing they try to *find a name* for what they do not "understand", and when they find a name they say they "understand". But to "find a name" does not mean to "understand". Unfortunately, people are usually satisfied with names. A man who knows a great many names, that is, a great many words, is deemed to understand a great deal – again excepting, of course, any sphere of practical activity wherein his ignorance very soon becomes evident.[3]

All this accumulation of information can end up by getting in the way. When I am teaching painting it sometimes happens that a pupil ceases to look at the thing he is painting and begins to do work below his usual standard. Almost invariably when I ask why he or she is no longer sensitive to what they are painting, I receive the answer that they read a book that told them that "flesh colour was always burnt sienna and white", or that "one shouldn't use small brushes". They were no longer looking for themselves and painting for themselves, but were stuck in someone else's theory.

We love theories and ideas, not just in painting but also in religion. It is so difficult to have to be simple, to open to what is there in front of you, to drop all preconceptions and paint from your raw gutsy self. If we collect many ideas, if we can talk knowledgeably about Comparative Religions; and compare intelligently the difference between Japanese and Tibetan Buddhism or discourse on the Symbolism of the Tarot, we might be listened to at dinner parties with admiration; but this is not at all the same as the experience of what religion is really about: the dropping of pretensions when we turn ourselves to God.

When I first saw this clearly, I wanted to forget that I had a mind, it seemed merely a temptation for me to try to be "clever" all the time. I resolved to be as simple as I could and try to serve

God that way. But I came to see that this attitude was not right either. God had given me a brain and I was meant to use it. There must be a balance. I needed all my intelligence to meet the difficulties that life presented, yet on the other hand the person that I was, my own "being", had to be worked on if I were to put my knowledge to good use.

> In Western culture it is considered that a man may possess great knowledge, for example he may be an able scientist, make discoveries, advance science, and at the same time he may be, and has the right to be, a petty, egoistic, caviling, mean, envious, vain, naïve, and absent-minded man. It seems to be considered here that a professor must always forget his umbrella everywhere.
>
> And yet it is his being. And people think that his knowledge does not depend on his being. People of Western culture put great value on the level of a man's knowledge but they do not value the level of a man's being and are not ashamed of the low level of their own being. They do not even understand what it means. And they do not understand that a man's knowledge depends on the level of his being . . .
>
> Knowledge by itself does not give understanding. Nor is understanding increased by an increase of knowledge alone. Understanding depends on the relation of knowledge to being. Understanding is the resultant of knowledge and being. And knowledge and being must not diverge too far, otherwise understanding will prove to be far removed from either. At the same time the relation of knowledge to being does not change with a mere growth of knowledge. It changes only when being grows simultaneously with knowledge. In other words, understanding grows only with the growth of being.[4]

Most of us are greedy for knowledge, but if we are not capable of assimilating it, it will not do us any good. Rumi, the great Sufi mystic, likens Wisdom to the supplies in a grocer's store. He has sugar in abundance, but he sees how much money each man has brought, and the capacity of his bag, and then measures out accordingly, one or two bushels. If a man has many bags and camels he is given a great deal. But if for another man the grocer considers one bushel enough the man is given no more, because that would be harmful to him.

The Tibetans say, "Knowledge must be burned, hammered, and beaten like pure gold. Then one can wear it as an ornament." Unless you can work with your knowledge, it is not really yours.

In the struggle to try to understand what we know, and think about what we understand, we develop ourselves, and each person finds the truth in the only way he can – by living it!

In trying to live according to the knowledge that I had studied, I found that my thoughts were very important. They had a life of their own, and I had to become responsible for them. If I wanted to go forward, I could not afford to remain stuck in stale heavy thoughts. Of course, negative and unpleasant thoughts were passing through my head all the time, but I found that if I did not agree with them and did not express them by speaking them in words, they would lose their power over me and disappear after a while. The experience of struggling with these thoughts showed me that it could be done, that it was possible to turn in another direction.

> All that we are is the result of what we have thought: it is founded on our thoughts, it is made up of our thoughts. If a man speaks or acts with evil thought, pain follows him, as the wheel follows the foot of the ox that draws the carriage.
>
> All that we are is the result of what we have thought: it is founded on our thoughts, it is made up of our thoughts. If a man speaks or acts with a pure thought, happiness follows him, like a shadow that never leaves him.
>
> "He abused me, he beat me, he defeated me, he robbed me – "In those who harbour such thoughts hatred will never cease.
>
> For hatred does not cease by hatred at any time: hatred ceases by love – this is an old rule.

> The world does not know that we must all come to an end here; but those who know it, their quarrels cease at once.[5]

> What you write with ink in small
black letters
Can all be lost through the work
of a single
drop
of
water.
But what is written
in your mind
is there
for
eternity.[6]

In a passage from Gurdjieff's book *Meetings with Remarkable Men*, a professor begs a monk to come to Europe to give his faith to the people there. The monk replies that faith cannot be given. It only arises in a man as a result of understanding. He tells the professor that even if his own beloved brother were to come and beg him to give him one tenth of his understanding, he could not do it, in spite of his ardent desire. To wish to do this is like wishing to fill someone with bread merely by looking at him.

> Understanding is required, from the totality of information intentionally learned and from personal experiencings;

whereas knowledge is only the automatic remembrance of words in a certain sequence.

Not only is it impossible, even with all one's desire, to give to another one's own inner understanding, formed in the course of life from the said factors, but also, as I recently established with certain other brothers of our monastery, there exists a law that the quality of what is perceived by anyone when another person tells him something, either for his knowledge or his understanding, depends on the quality of the data formed in the person speaking.[7]

To illustrate what he has just said, the monk tells about two very old and venerable monks who come to his monastery to give sermons. The first monk, Brother Sez, speaks so beautifully that everyone listens entranced. Brother Ahl on the other hand speaks badly and indistinctly because of his great age. However,

The stronger the impression made at the moment by the words of Brother Sez, the more this impression evaporates, until there ultimately remains in the hearer nothing at all.

But in the case of Brother Ahl, although at first what he says makes almost no impression, later, the gist of it takes on a definite form, more and more each day, and is instilled as a whole into the heart and remains there for ever.

When we became aware of this and began trying to discover why it was so, we came to the unanimous conclusion that the sermons of Brother Sez proceeded only from his mind, and therefore acted on our minds, whereas those of Brother Ahl proceeded from his being and acted on our being . . .

Only understanding can lead to being, whereas knowledge is but a passing presence in it. New knowledge displaces the old and the result is, as it were, a pouring from the empty into the void.

One must strive to understand; this alone can lead to our Lord God.[8]

> Truth and lie do not allude to the truth and falsehood of things themselves, but to a pronouncement of the soul. The soul pledges itself to the truth or to the lie. Human truth is a verification by man's being true.[9]

Everything that I had studied showed me that I had to try to begin to live the truth rather than learn it. But how could this be done? If truth is only verified by a man's being true, then where was my truth? When I looked inside myself I could not find anything but an assortment of conflicting hopes, desires, fears . . . How could I pick what was true from that mixture? I had to begin the search for truth by seeing the truth in myself first . . .

3

To See Ourselves as Others See Us

Robert Burns's poem says:

O wad someone the giftie gi' us
tae see ourselves as others see us.

But I always thought he could keep his giftie – the last thing I wanted to know was what other people thought of me; I had an uneasy suspicion that it wouldn't be flattering to my ego!

My feelings were justified one day when a group of us were asked to talk in front of a video camera. When the film was played back and I saw myself on the screen I was horrified. That show-off, posturing and peacocking in front of the camera, surely that couldn't be me!

That video left a lasting impression. It showed me what it was in me that used to irritate certain people. I had never been aware of this before! Once I started looking at myself more objectively I saw that there were undesirable elements in myself which were coming out because I was blind to their existence. I saw that other people were in the same position; acting equally blindly because they were not seeing certain aspects of themselves.

Jung tells us that it is necessary to ponder over our actions and motives. This is not at all the same thing as brooding – which just goes round and round in a circle and leads nowhere. When you are depressed about your faults it is important to make yourself the object of serious study. Unless we do this we cannot grow.

> If you have done something that puzzles you and you ask yourself what could have prompted you to such an action, you need the sting of a bad conscience and its discriminating faculty in order to discover the real motive of your behaviour. It is only then that you can see what motives are governing your actions. The sting of a bad conscience even spurs you on to discover things that were unconscious before, and in this way you may be able to cross the threshold of the unconscious and take cognizance of those impersonal forces which make you an unconscious instrument of the wholesale murderer in man. . . .
>
> Self-knowledge, in the form of an examination of conscience, is demanded by Christian ethics. They were very pious people who maintained that self-knowledge paves the way to knowledge of God.[1]

When one discovers something unpleasant about oneself, the first thing one is tempted to do is to blame external circumstances: "If my spouse or parent were not so unkind, or critical, I would be better tempered." Or "If I had more money", or "If I could get away." Jung however, tells us that this is not so.

> Unless you change yourself inwardly too, outward changes in the situation are either worthless or actually harmful.[2]

Maurice Nicoll, Jung's pupil, agrees with this view.

> Here is a man, for example, who has suddenly acquired a lot of money. He packs his trunks and goes abroad and imagines that everything is going to be different. But everything will be just the same after a time. He will be as suspicious as before, as quarrelsome as before, as negative and upset as before. And this is because he himself has not changed. So he will attract the same kind of events, the same kind of situations. . . . the whole secret is, not to try to change external circumstances, because if you do not

> change yourself and the way you take the repeating events of life, everything will recur in the same way. You will get mad, distracted, upset, bitter, angry, just in the same way as you always have to every recurring event of life. You will react to them all in the same way because you are what you are.[3]

But of course, self-knowledge is not easily come by. It is easy to fool oneself, and that is why spiritual direction from the right teacher is so important. Over the years all of us have developed certain habits in dealing with the outside world. We have developed a mask, an outward personality, which is protecting the real vulnerable self, our essence, which is the true part of us and the only point from which growth is possible.

> Some people say that they do observe themselves. They say: "I see that I do this and I do that", and think that is all that is necessary. I would say that this is the first step certainly, but that you must begin to *dislike* behaving in this way, and it is just this dislike of yourself, which strikes at the root of your self-admiration or self-love, that is the beginning of making Personality less active and therefore Essence less passive. To justify what you observe is quite useless. Something has to pull you up sooner or later. That is, another emotion apart from self-love must begin in you and this emotion belongs to the nourishment of Essence.[4]

Martin Buber, speaking from the Hasidic Tradition, corroborates this view:

> The origin of all conflict between me and my fellow men is that I do not say what I mean, and that I do not do what I say. . . . By our contradiction, our lie, we foster conflict-situations and give them power over us until they enslave

us. From here, there is no way out but by the crucial realization: everything depends on myself, and the crucial decision: I will straighten myself out.

But in order that a man may be capable of this great feat, he must first find his way from the casual, accessory elements of his existence to his own self; he must find his own self, not the trivial ego of the egotistic individual, but the deeper self of the person living in a relationship to the world. And that is also contrary to everything we are accustomed to.[5]

Cecil Lewis, in his book *A Way to Be*, writes that we are given at birth an inner mirror, more difficult and more painful to look into than the one hanging in the hallway. But if we dare to look into it, it can reflect everything we are. In each of us is a multitude of different people. Within us lives the saint, the sinner, the honest man, the liar, the wise man and the fool. With our mirror we can learn to see them all and catch the chaos of the state we are in: and the struggle can begin.

How can we help ourselves if we don't know what needs help? We need to see. We may be less than we thought we were, but we are also more. Our mirror stops us lying to ourselves and we feel clean.

And what a change such an admission of frailty could bring into our lives! For out of it can grow humility and a readiness to serve. From service grows responsibility and with that begins the birth of Conscience – which is the representative of the Creator in us. And it is the rebirth of Conscience, through our growing consciousness, that holds true objective hope for the world to come.

Turn then to your inner mirror, which, if you persist, will show you all you need to know. It is not an easy road; but as long as you tread it, you will be in a state of grace.[6]

Our mirror can help us to work on ourselves right now, this very moment. Usually when something touches our conscience it is easy to say "Tomorrow I'll go on a retreat", or "Tomorrow I'll pray", just as we say "Tomorrow I'll go on a diet!" Trungpa says

> Generally we tend to prepare too much. We say, "once I make a lot of money, then I will go somewhere to study and meditate and become a priest", or whatever it is we would like to become. But we never do it on the spot. We always speak in terms of, "Once I do something, then . . ." We always plan too much. We want to change our lives rather than use our lives, the present moment, as part of the practice, and this hesitation on our part creates a lot of setbacks in our spiritual practice. Most of us have romantic ideas – "I'm bad now but one day, when I change, I'll be good."[7]

Observing myself in the right way was not as easy as I had thought at first. For example, if I felt myself to be in a state of religious fervour, I would accept this as being good; but then I began to see that this might be a form of indulgence.

Martin Buber describes being transported one morning in a religious ecstasy, and earthly things seemed by contrast of no importance. Then he was interrupted by a visit from an unknown young man. Buber was friendly and talked kindly to the young man, but he was not there in spirit. Later on he learned that the young man had left him to commit suicide.

> I learned that he had come to me not casually, but borne by destiny, not for a chat but for a decision. He had come to me, he had come in this hour. What do we expect when we are in despair and yet go to a man? Surely a presence by means of which we are told that nevertheless there is meaning.
>
> Since then I have given up the "religious" which is nothing but the exception, extraction, exaltation, ecstasy; or it has given me up. I possess nothing but the everyday out of which I am never taken . . . I know no fulness but

> each mortal hour's fulness of claim and responsibility. Though far from being equal to it, yet I know that in the claim I am claimed and may respond in responsibility, and know who speaks and demands a response.[8]

Buber's story made a great impression on me. It showed me that the important thing was to be here now, to be available to what Life was asking of me. Having made the inner commitment, the chief difficulty was to remember. To remember not just as a vague thought in my head, but to remember with my whole being, so that each remembering was a new bringing to birth of that real self that God was calling me to be.

On the way to seeing myself I was often discouraged. Sometimes I would see someone I admired and want to be like her or him. One morning I was walking back from church, thinking how much I wanted to be like my friend, the singer Mary O'Hara instead of myself. Then I seemed to wake up, and became aware of the beautiful tree ahead of me, and the grass around it. I imagined each piece of grass wanting to be a tree, and the horrible tangled mess that would result if each blade of grass had its wish. God already had one person like Mary, He didn't need another clone. Meanwhile, who was to be Brigid if I refused to be myself? It was just me I was called on to be, and my own inner universe that I was called on to redeem.

The Rabbi Zusya said, shortly before he died, "In the world to come I shall not be asked: 'Why were you not Moses?' but 'Why were you not Zusya?' "

Every individual's development is of infinite importance because each of us reflects God in a unique way. The only chance for the development of mankind is the development of each person as himself. It is not our job to look at the life of another person and try to copy it.

> It would only be misleading to study the achievements of another man and endeavour to equal him; for in so doing, a man would miss precisely what he and he alone is called upon to do. The Baal-Shem said: "Every man should behave according to his 'rung'. If he does not, if he seizes the 'rung' of a fellow man and abandons his own, he will actualize neither the one nor the other." thus, the way by which a man can reach God is revealed to him only through the knowledge of his own being, the knowledge of his essential quality and inclination. 'Everything has in him something precious that is in no one else."[9]

> Now you shall hear how a man may become perfect, if he devotes himself to the work which is natural to him.
>
> A man's own natural duty, even if it seems imperfectly done, is better than work not naturally his own, even if this is well performed. When a man acts according to the law of his nature, he cannot be sinning.[10]

4

Evil

When I was a teenager the nuns in my convent school used to warn us girls about the evilness of men. We learned that they were ravening wolves, bent on taking advantage of our innocence. I used to picture them all roistering in taverns with duelling scars on their cheeks and wearing black capes. In drunken frenzy they would vow to each other to seduce us.

It was a terrible disappointment when I began to go out with a few men to discover that they were just ordinary people like me! Later when I did encounter something in people which felt evil, I was always struck by its smallness and meanness – there was none of the grandeur of the swirling black capes!

> The Evil inclination is like one who runs about the world keeping his hand closed. Nobody knows what he has inside it. He goes up to everyone and asks: "What do you suppose I have in my hand?" And every person thinks that just what he wants most of all is hidden there. And everyone runs after the Evil Inclination. Then he opens his hand, and it is empty.[1]

As I grew older and began to understand more I saw that the reason that I had been so fascinated by the idea of evil was that I had hidden the evil in myself. From Jung's writings I learned that no one is entirely "good". We all have a "shadow" self which, if not recognized, gathers force underground and can erupt later and do damage. It is necessary to become more aware of the dark and hidden side of one's nature.

> Good does not become better by being exaggerated, but worse, and a small evil becomes a big one through being disregarded and repressed. The shadow is very much a part of human nature, and it is only at night that no shadows exist.[2]

The first duty, then, would seem that we must let ourselves see the evil in ourselves, and not turn away or go on blindly, pushing away the uneasy feeling that all may not be well.

> When Evil is made conscious it is no longer the same evil, because it is said that "All evil is unconscious".[3]

When I first read that all evil is unconscious, I could not believe it and wanted to test this saying. I watched myself and others, and gradually became convinced that this was true. I had thought that someone like Hitler might be aware of the evil he was doing, but then I heard a story that Hitler went to see a village that he had ordered to be razed to the ground, and the people in it murdered; he stood looking at it and wept, saying, "How evil these people must have been to make me do this to them!"

Laurens van der Post describes the mechanics of this turning away from the truth of what one is doing, which he experienced while in a Japanese Prisoner-of-War camp.

> We had all been beaten up for no apparent reason. As always when this happened, I had noticed a strange, unseeing look in the eyes of the Japanese. It was focused not at us but at something beyond us. Were they afraid that, should their eyes focus on us, they would recognize our common humanity, and so the cruelties they were inflicting would not only be challenged but extinguished?
>
> Yet there was again something extraordinarily familiar to me about this look. Where had I seen it before? In the eyes of my men and fellow officers there was an expression of utter bewilderment. Yet that, too, seemed just as familiar

> to me as the look on the Japanese faces. Then suddenly I had it! I had seen that look of bewilderment so often in the law courts of my native South Africa when some black native countryman was being tried in a language he could not understand, and for a breach of laws that often he did not even know existed. And even when he did know of their existence he certainly had no understanding of the assumptions that served as their justification. The judges too, in passing sentence, rarely looked at the uncomprehending accused. Their eyes too were generally focused on some abstract of vision beyond the ragged and tattered creature in the dock, as if afraid that one glance would deprive him of his capacity for passing judgement.[4]

As Jung points out – our only hope is to try to become more aware:

> The hero's main feat is to overcome the monster of darkness: it is the long-hoped-for and expected triumph of consciousness over the unconscious. The coming of consciousness was probably the most tremendous experience of primeval times, for with it a world came into being whose existence no one had suspected before. "And God said, 'Let there be light'" is the projection of that immemorial experience of the separation of consciousness from the unconscious.[5]

Martin Buber sheds a light on the question of good and evil by pointing out that the only choice or direction that we can actively choose, is towards the good. Evil is merely a series of grabbing at whatever appears desirable at the moment, so it is lack of direction; and as desires are legion so the devil is legion:

> Evil cannot be done with the whole soul; good can only be done with the whole soul. It is done when the soul's

rapture, proceeding from its highest forces, seizes upon all the forces and plunges them into the purging and transmuting fire, as into the mightiness of decision. Evil is lack of direction and that which is done in it and out of it as the grasping, seizing, devouring, compelling, seducing, exploiting, humiliating, torturing and destroying of what offers itself. Good is direction and what is done in it; that which is done in it is done with the whole soul, so that in fact all the vigour and passion with which evil might have been done is included in it.[6]

Once we have seen the need for aim and the value of it, aim can be trained. It can grow in us. Usually we set ourselves aims far too big for our powers – and far too vague. So we fail to carry them out and become discouraged. The way to train ourselves in aim is to have a small one, but *carry it through*. This is what is important.

A man may have a long-term aim to be a millionaire; but he must start by saving a penny a day. If he does this, he gains confidence and strength. He has established a principle. If he just dreams of wealth, as most of us do, he is unlikely to get it.[7]

I had a personal experience of using evil energy to help me, when I was overcome with anger. I had always had a capacity for great anger, even as a child. When I was a little girl I hit my younger brother over the head with the metal end of the garden hosepipe. I cut him badly, and if it had been something heavier I might have injured him. I wasn't sorry either, especially after I had been spanked for it. A murderous rage had come over me: I literally "saw red". I did feel guilty though, and the memory returned whenever a fit of rage would come over me. I hated the ugliness of my temper – I wanted to present a pretty picture, even to myself. It made the world around me ugly, too.

> When we experience aggression we feel that everything is an expression of injustice. There is too much concrete, too much steel, too much grease, too much pollution, and we feel very angry and frustrated. We are so involved with this world of emotions that, although we might have a beautiful sunny day, fantastic weather, and a fantastic view, we still grind our teeth. We feel that the world is trying to mock us. The clear blue sky is trying to mock us or insult us. The beautiful sunshine is embarrassing to look at, and the fantastic full moon and the beautiful clouds around it are an insult. There is constant hate, enormous hate, so much so that it is almost unreal. We feel that we are actually levitating off the ground because we are so angry. We feel that our feet are not attached to the ground, that we are hovering above the world, because there is such a sense of aggression taking place.[8]

Then one day it dawned on me that something in myself was holding on to this anger, even enjoying it!

> It must be admitted that a fit of rage or a sulk has its secret attractions. Were that not so, most people would long since have acquired a little wisdom.[9]

When I read Trungpa's description of the energy of anger as "wonderful manure" which could be used to grow lovely crops, I began to understand that this energy could be used. I would first have to give up the enjoyment of my anger, though, and see it for what it was.

> When you have this hostile attitude and try to suppress things, then each time you knock one thing out another

> springs up in its place, and when you attack that one, another one comes up from somewhere else. There is the continual trick of the Ego, so that when you try to disentangle one part of the knot you pull on the string and only make it tighter somewhere else, so you are continually trapped in it. Therefore the thing is not to battle any more, not to try and sort out the bad things and only achieve good, but respect them and acknowledge them.[10]

One morning I was upset by someone close to me. I felt I had been badly treated, and the feeling of rage and anger possessed me. Suddenly the thought came to me – could I really use the force in this anger for something?

There was an idea for a painting that I had been thinking over for some time but had not got around to doing . . . I went into my studio and started work. The painting progressed quickly and well, and two hours later I woke up to the fact that I had been at peace all that time; not tormented with my own enraged thoughts. Moreover, I was still bubbling with energy! My anger did return again, but I had found a way of helping to cope with it; any activity would serve the same purpose; the main thing was not to express the angry thoughts or they would grow.

To my surprise, when I later read *The Tibetan Book of the Dead* I found a passage which states specifically that wrathful energy can be transformed into creative energy. I felt as if my discovery had been confirmed!

After that, a feeling of anger was a signal for me to do something active – paint or mow the lawn. I tried at the same time to occupy my mind with something useful instead of allowing my thoughts to revolve endlessly around the source of my anger. This is not the same as suppressing the anger. An important factor is the seeing of the anger for what it is – then not allowing it to take hold of me.

> If we are capable of maintaining attention, not by will but by perception, by seeing the fact and remaining with the fact without any movement away from it, then the fact

undergoes a radical change. You can see this if you do it. That is, if I remain completely with violence, not trying to do something about it, because I am violent, then in the very attention you give to that factor of sensation which is called violence, it disappears. When there is this light of attention on it violence disappears completely, for ever. If you do it you will discover it for yourself.[11]

You do not have to keep calm and suppress the energy of anger, but you can transform your aggression into dynamic energy. It is a question of how open you are, how much you are really willing to do it. If there is less fascination and satisfaction with the explosion and release of your energy, then there is more likelihood of transmuting it . . . You do not have to completely change yourself, but you can use part of your energy in an awakened state.[12]

One shall not kill "the evil impulse", the passion, in oneself, but one shall serve God *with it*; it is the power which is destined to receive its direction from man.[13]

I knew that in painting a picture the dark shadows are needed to display the light. Darkness has a legitimate place. It can supply energy. An Eastern proverb says: "An angel sits on your right shoulder and a devil on your left, and in the friction between the two we make our souls."

5

Talking

I've always loved talking. My mother told me that as a baby I was late in walking, and had to be carried all the time, but talking incessantly! This characteristic, unfortunately, has not been much curtailed over the years.

I used to believe that talking things over would solve problems. If someone had lost their faith, I would argue with them for hours, but somehow nothing seemed to come of this.

One day I was asked to observe unnecessary talking. All the next day I tried to listen to myself, and I heard this ceaseless waterfall of words; but I went back and said, "It all seemed necessary!"

Then I made a resolution. I picked a time when I was going to say as little as possible, but unfortunately I was unexpectedly asked to a party at that very time. I stuck to my resolution, but was afraid that my silence would give offence. I needn't have worried. Nobody even noticed my silence – they were too busy talking themselves!

There is an Eastern tale about a certain Mullah Nasrudin who went to the market and saw some birds being sold for a great deal of money. Very excited, he rushed home and brought back his pet hen. But nobody offered him very much money for it. He shouted angrily, "This is a disgrace! You are selling birds only one half the size of my hen at ten times the price!" Someone told him, "Mullah, the other birds were parrots, they are talking birds. They are worth more because they can talk."

> "Fool!" said Nasrudin, "those birds you value only because they can talk. This one, which has wonderful thoughts and yet does not annoy people with chatter, you reject."[1]

Krishnamurti noted a curious similarity between gossip and worry: they were both the outcome of a restlessness of mind which had to be occupied all the time with passing interests, and new sensations. Gossip, by talking about another, is an escape from oneself. People take this escape route all the time, by talking about the neighbours or by reading the papers, with their gossip columns and stories of divorce and murder. The more we are distracted by such things, the less tranquil our mind becomes. We become incapable of real search and inquiry.

> Gossip is an expression of a restless mind; but merely to be silent does not indicate a tranquil mind. Tranquillity does not come into being with abstinence or denial; it comes with the understanding of what it *is*.
>
> If we did not worry, most of us would feel that we were not alive; to be struggling with a problem is for the majority of us an indication of existence. The constant tension over a problem which thought itself has created only dulls the mind, making it insensitive and weary.
>
> Why is there this ceaseless preoccupation with a problem? Will worry resolve the problem? Or does the answer to the problem come when the mind is quiet? But for most people, a quiet mind is a rather fearsome thing; they are afraid to be quiet, for heaven knows what they may discover in themselves, and worry is a preventive.
>
> Gossip and worry can come to an end only when the restlessness of the mind is understood. Mere abstinence, control or discipline will not bring about tranquillity, but only dull the mind, making it insensitive and confined.
>
> Curiosity is not the way of understanding. Understanding comes with self-knowledge. . . . Speculation, like curiosity, is an indication of restlessness; and a restless mind, however gifted, destroys understanding and happiness.[2]

In *Among the Dervishes* a Sufi tells the author of the danger to the Westerner of believing too much in words;

> The people have been trained to believe that anything that can be *done* is either inborn – like a talent – or can be learned by the *stringing together of a number of words*. This is one of the grossest impositions which have ever been perpetrated.

Words used for their own sake eventually cease to have any meaning. They become no longer connected to any real experience.

> . . . sentiments when once they have been expressed, become what we call "worn out". They become truisms; things repeated mechanically. They are tags, and they have tags attached to them. People carry on whole conversations in proverbs. But they are not *living* the proverbs. Proverbs and truisms are for this reason dangerous, because they produce blindness or non-thought. When you get a principle on which everyone is agreed, you get the beginning of complacency and deterioration. Nobody will oppose the principle of "peace for all the world". Believing that they believe in this, they have to do nothing about it. Oh, yes, I know that they talk about it, keep the matter in the headlines. But they do not apply the essential character of peace to themselves as individuals. They now regard "peace" as something which applies to groups of people, not to the individual. This is why there can be no real peace, only the absence of actual fighting. But peace is more than that.[3]

Because words have ceased to convey real meaning, we lose the habit of responding to them. And yet Buber tells us that it is our responsibility to respond. We must face each situation as it happens; I must hear another's words as directed precisely at me. Sometimes the responding may be a letting go rather than a going forward towards the speaker, but if we are present at the moment listening with our whole self, the response will be honest and the right one for us to make;

> Nor are we now finished with it, we have to give up that expectation: a situation of which we have become aware is never finished with, but we subdue it into the substance of lived life. Only then, true to the moment, do we experience a life that is something other than a sum of moments. We respond to the moment, but at the same time we respond on its behalf, we answer for it. A newly-created concrete reality has been laid in our arms; we answer for it. A dog has looked at you, you answer for its glance, a child has clutched your hand, you answer for its touch, a host of men moves about you, you answer for their need.

In human relationships words are not always what can help. I had a pupil of whom I was very fond, but we had a disagreement, and I felt that she was in the wrong. I was on my way to see her, to argue with her and point out where I felt she was at fault, when something made me stop for a moment and I began to pray about the situation, thinking of the girl all the time. Suddenly it seemed to me that I was the girl. I began to perceive the world in a different way, through groping instinct, instead of through the head. For a second it seemed that my body received the sights and sounds around me with delicate antennae infinitely more sensitive than a dogmatic mind. I saw how words would come to such a person, hitting her like stones, even if they were true. What was needed was a sensitivity without words. I went to her in a different spirit, without saying anything, and the problem resolved itself.

> . . . with listening, the ego all too frequently gets in the way. This explains why so many conversations are exercises in talking at, rather than with, one another. Not only do we prefer the sound of our own voice, we prefer also the procession of our own thoughts. We tend to be more interested in what we are going to say next than in what someone else is saying now. When this tendency gets out of hand the consequences are painfully familiar: we become bores, we look to others mainly to provide us with a cue

for our own remarks. Having lost interest in drawing others out so that they speak their minds, we neither get to know nor learn anything from them.[5]

I began to see that I believed too much in words. Words cannot take the place of experience that has been lived through, but it's very easy to believe in them. If, for example, I know the name for something, I often think I know the thing itself.

The danger that faces us today is that the whole of reality will be replaced by words. This accounts for that terrible lack of instinct in modern man, particularly the city-dweller. He lacks all contact with life and the breath of nature. He knows a rabbit or a cow only from the illustrated paper, the dictionary, or the movies, and thinks he knows what it is really like – and is then amazed that cowsheds "smell", because the dictionary didn't say so.[6]

Ouspensky tells us that when some pupils of Gurdjieff tried to become more aware, and struggle with their habits, they found that talking was the habit that most got in their way:

No one saw this habit in himself, no one could struggle with it because it was always connected with some characteristic which the man considered to be positive in himself. Either he wanted to be "sincere", or he wanted to know what another man thought, or he wanted to help someone by speaking of himself or of others, and so on, and so on.

I very soon saw that the struggle with the habit of talking, of speaking, in general, more than is necessary, could become the centre of gravity of work on oneself because this habit touched everything, penetrated everything, and was for many people the least noticed. It was very curious to observe how this habit (I say "habit" simply for lack of another word, it would be more correct to say "this sin" or "this misfortune") at once took possession of everything no matter what a man might begin to do.

It was suggested that everyone should keep absolute silence for a time as a discipline, but Gurdjieff told them that complete silence was easier than the real struggle in life; which is to say only what is necessary:

> The whole point is that we say a good deal too much. If we limited ourselves to what is actually necessary, this alone would be keeping silence. And it is the same with everything else, with food, with pleasures, with sleep; with everything there is a limit to what is necessary. After this "sin" begins. This is something that must be grasped, a "sin" is something which is not necessary.[7]

I began to discover that of course there are moments when it is very important to speak, and to find the right and healing word. But it is so easy to believe too much in words. My mother told me that for years she had been annoyed at my father because he didn't talk a lot. "I wanted us to have wonderful conversations together," she told me, "and I used to feel that we were not communicating. But now I am so grateful for our companionable silence together, and I would hate to have a man who chattered all the time."

> Words are the pretext. It is the element of congeneity that draws one man to another, not words. If a man should see a hundred thousand miracles and expositions and divine graces, if there is no element of congeneity in him connecting him with the prophet or the saint concerned, then all those phenomena will be profitless.[8]

The speech of created beings is with sounds. The word of God is silence. God's secret word of love can be nothing else but silence. Christ is the silence of God.

Just as there is no tree like the Cross, so there is no harmony like the silence of God. The Pythagoreans discerned this harmony in the fathomless eternal silence around the stars. In this world, necessity is the vibration of God's silence.

Our soul is constantly clamorous with noise, but there is one point in it which is silence, and which we never hear. When the silence of God comes to the soul and penetrates it and joins the silence which is secretly present in us, from then on we have our treasure and our heart in God; and space opens before us as the opening fruit of a plant divides in two, for we are seeing the universe from a point situated outside space.[9]

6

Helping People

When I was younger I was keen on helping people. I would sacrifice a lot of time and effort on someone, but often the whole thing ended in disaster, and the one I had wanted to help ended up disliking me. I never could understand this. Surely, even if I had been a little heavy-handed, the recipient of my good-will should have been pleased, at least at my good intentions?

It took a very unpleasant experience to show me the truth of the situation. I had brought my son to hospital after he had taken an overdose – he was handicapped and had decided that he did not want to live any more. I was told to sit in the waiting room until they could tell me whether there was any hope or not. I was numbed with anxiety and grief, and sat staring at the opposite wall alone, until two women entered the room. The first, a pale composed woman, I recognized instantly as being in the same state as I was. The second woman was middle aged and well dressed, with a florid complexion. She clutched the hand of the first woman tightly. Several times I saw the first woman make an effort to remove her hand, but in vain. The older woman caught my eye and beamed a significant glance of pity on to the pale woman, who was staring ahead without speaking. At last a nurse came and called her, and she extricated herself with a look of unspeakable relief.

Looking as if a choice morsel had been taken away from her, the florid woman now came and sat in the chair next to mine.

"I've been helping her", she confided in me. "You see, her husband's very ill and she knows no one here, so I offered my help. When my daughter fell off her horse and got concussion,

I vowed that I would help people if she recovered, so here I am! I'm just a shoulder to cry on for people in trouble!" She leaned over and peered into my face. "Are you in trouble, dear?" She grabbed my hand before I could say anything, and I felt suffocated. I couldn't cope with her, and was too weak inside to fend her off. I began to feel that I couldn't breathe, and was only rescued by the nurse calling me into the ward. My son recovered that time, but that moment of unwanted help continued to haunt me. I saw that good intentions weren't enough. It dawned on me that there was a lot more going on under the guise of helping, much more concealed emotion than most of us are prepared to face.

Chogyam Trungpa tells us that the idea of helping people is more subtle than we realize. Often in trying to help people we make a nuisance of ourselves. We want to be important so we force ourselves on the other person.

> We march straight through into another person's territory, disregarding the proper conditions for entering it. There might be signs saying, "Keep off the grass, no trespassing". But each time we see these signs, they make us more aggressive, more revolutionary. We just push ourselves into the other person's territory, like a tank going through a wall. We are not only committing vandalism to someone else's territory, but we are disrupting our own territory as well – it is inward vandalism too. It is being a nuisance to ourselves as well as to others.[1]

We don't want to think that we are a nuisance to people but the answer is not just to be polite and put on a genteel manner. We must use all our energy and intelligence. We have to open to others, without trying to magnetize or repel. We must be tentative. It takes a long time to learn how to open – to put aside our defences. The first step is to begin learning how to love ourselves – to make friends with ourselves. The second step is to learn how to communicate with others and gradually help them. This takes a long time and much disciplined patience. Only then are we ready to help without selfishness.

> Usually when we help someone, we are looking for something in return. We might say to our children, "I want you to be happy, therefore I'm putting all my energy into you", which implies that "I want you to be happy because I want you to provide me with entertainment; bring me happiness, because I want to be happy." In the third stage of selfless help, true compassion, we do not do things because it gives us pleasure but because things need to be done. Our response is selfless, noncentralized. It is not for them or for me. It is environmental generosity.
>
> But we cannot just go out and try to practise this kind of compassion. First we must learn how not to make a nuisance of ourselves. If we can make friends with ourselves, if we are willing to be what we are, without hating parts of ourselves and trying to hide them, then we can begin to open to others. And if we can begin to open without always having to protect ourselves, then perhaps we can begin to really help others.[2]

To accept help can require as much tact as to give it. There is a story about a wise man called Abdullah ben Yahya, who was showing to a visitor a manuscript he had written. The man pointed to a word which he said had been mis-spelt. Abdullah at once altered the word, and the visitor left, very pleased with himself. An onlooker asked Abdullah why he had changed the word, considering that the first version was right and the correction was wrong. Abdullah said, "The visitor thought he was helping. It was a social occasion and I applied the rule of politeness and not truth. If this man had been my student it would have been a different matter."

> Only stupid people and pedants imagine that their duty is to instruct everyone, when the motive of the people is generally not to seek instruction, but to attract attention.[3]

I found this story very illuminating. There are many occasions when it is important to apply the rule of politeness and not that of truth. It is a question of when to use what you know. One can be sensitive to where people are – what they are ready to hear. One can allow people space and time; to let them make their own mistakes if necessary.

Most doctors know this; they know that if someone is dying, it is better not to confront them baldly with the truth, but wait until they are ready to hear it. I remember the horror of the moment when I was told, without preparation, that my five-year-old son was schizophrenic. The shock did terrible damage to me, and it was not necessary. I would have learned of my son's difficulties as time went on, and have been more ready to accept them as I grew older. Perhaps that psychiatrist thought he was helping by making me face the truth, but it was his lack of sensitivity in our suffering that was, and still is even now, as I recall that moment, extremely painful.

That psychiatrist was living in his own world, where we were just part of his routine job. The truth is that we are all living in our own worlds – a universe with ourselves as the central point. I am always the main character in my own drama; that is why in playing Cinderella, I have to be so careful not to reduce other people to the role of Ugly Sister.

The lady at the hospital was playing Lady Bountiful, and had cast me in the role of grateful beggar. If I had not been so exhausted emotionally I would have been angry; except for the fact that I saw that this was what I had been doing to other people all my life.

I began to wonder what was behind the wish to help people. Was it that I needed to prove to myself that I was good? And if so, why did I have to prove that I was good all the time, unless there was a secret fear that I was bad? I needed grateful people around me to reassure myself. Sometimes in order to achieve this I would strain at great self-sacrifice, and then resent it! I was spending more than I had in my spiritual bank. I would make offers to help people with money or time, then be annoyed if they accepted, and I was left with no money for myself. Then I would dislike them, or get someone else to give them help instead, thus involving other people in my charities.

> A man decides to give away his last shirt, but instead, he strips of his last shirt the man to whom he meant to give his own. Or he decides to give away his own shirt but gives away somebody else's and is offended if somebody refuses to give him his shirt so that he may give it to another. This is what happens most often.[4]

There was a kind of unconscious "backlash" going on, something in me was not agreeing to all this niceness, and was taking its revenge.

> We all have a great need to be good ourselves, and occasionally we like to show it by the appropriate actions. If good can come of evil self-interest then the two sides of human nature have co-operated. But when in a fit of enthusiasm we begin with the good, our deep-rooted selfishness remains in the background, unsatisfied and resentful, only waiting for an opportunity to take its revenge in the most atrocious way.[5]

I found that I did better when I helped people in such a way that my own interest was also served. Gurdjieff said once, "Always endeavouur to do what is useful to others and agreeable to ourselves." When I did that I avoided the reaction of my "shadow self". Later I found that it was possible to give altruistically, providing that I was aware when I gave. If I were conscious of my own destructive needs I could take them into account. Then I would not be giving or helping compulsively, to satisfy my secret guilt, but giving because the other person was in some way also myself. This would mean that the other person is left free; because sometimes helping can be a way of trying to control people, bringing them into our own universe and expanding it in that way.

Shunryu Suzuki, a Japanese teacher of Zen, shows that learning not to try to control people by force can also help us in our own attempt at prayer or meditation (sitting in meditation is called *zazen* in Japanese).

> Even though you try to put people under some control, it is impossible. You cannot do it. The best way to control people is to encourage them to be mischievous. Then they will be in control in its wider sense. To give your sheep or cow a large, spacious meadow is the way to control him. So it is with people: first let them do what they want, and watch them. This is the best policy. To ignore them is not good; that is the worst policy. The second worst is trying to control them. The best one is to watch them, just to watch them, without trying to control them.
>
> The same way works for you yourself as well. If you want to obtain perfect calmness in your *zazen*, you should not be bothered by the various images you find in your mind. Let them come, and let them go. Then they will be under control . . . The true purpose is to see things as they are, to observe things as they are, and to let everything go as it goes. This is to put everything under control in its widest sense.[6]

When my husband left us to work abroad, the boys were just reaching adolescence. I realized that as a mother and a woman I would soon not be able to give orders to them any more. In any case, I wanted them to be men, and not "Mummy's boys".

I decided to begin treating them as if they were already men. When a difficult situation came up, we discussed it together, each giving our own point of view. The right course of action then would emerge from the discussion. In that way their transition from boys to men was very smooth, we had few arguments because they felt that I respected them.

This showed me that when I had been trying before to manipulate people by "helping them", there had been a lack of respect. One of the worst things you can do to people is not to respect them. In the East it is a terrible thing to make someone "lose face". Each person is a separate universe; their universe can only be redeemed by themselves. Sometimes, I can help a little, but with great care; the other person is not me!

In order to help the other it is important to know one's own universe thoroughly, particularly the dark side of it. After the first shock of seeing my evil side, the important thing was to go on facing it – not to paper over the cracks. So often I had felt superior when helping people. But by seeing the truth of what I am, I see that I am not superior; I'm the same as everyone else. If I really want to help I have to make some effort on my being.

I remember an Austrian leader of a mountain rescue team, coming back after someone had fallen down a mountain. He remarked how many people had wanted to help, and were only a nuisance. "When someone is in trouble on a mountain," he said, "everyone wants to help, but they don't know what to do and end up needing rescuing themselves. Only someone who has put years of effort and self-discipline into being trained can really help."

I felt that this was a good reason to work on myself – the aim that eventually I might really help someone.

I am dead because I lack desire;
I lack desire because I think I possess;
I think I possess because I do not try to give.
In trying to give, you see that you have nothing;
Seeing you have nothing, you try to give of yourself;
Trying to give of yourself, you see that you are nothing;
Seeing you are nothing, you desire to become;
In desiring to become, you begin to live.[7]

7
Love

In the matter of love it is hard to become an adult. As children most of us are loved just for being what we are. When I grew up, I still wanted love to go on pouring over me, like an unturned off tap. I didn't think that I had to earn it.

I had a lot of emotion going on inside me, which I called love, but I didn't stand back and look at it. From my own point of view I was very reasonable, all I wanted was to love and be loved: all I wanted was to be happy. I hadn't realized that there could be more to the whole thing than that. What I hadn't seen was that I was still acting like a baby. I hadn't taken responsibility for myself. I wanted love in order to put the responsibility for my happiness on to someone else.

The first thing that I had to learn was to be responsible for my own happiness. I had to develop myself into the kind of person I could rely on in order to stop clutching at other people all the time. Otherwise the quality of what I offered as love would be worth nothing.

Trungpa says that we often have a grasping approach to love. To get security we like to regard ourselves as helpless babies and "leap into someone's lap".

Alternatively we might regard someone else as being our baby. There is a powerful urge to belong, to be someone's child or to have them be our child. This can happen with our relationship to an organization too. We can nurse it and help it grow, or it can be the great mother, and feed us continually. These two patterns run through any form of energy that we occupy ourselves with – a friendship or a career; either we want to control it or we want to be part of it.

> However, there is another kind of love and compassion, a third way. Just be what you are. You do not reduce yourself to the level of an infant nor do you demand that another person leap into your lap. You simply be what you are in the world, in life. If you can be what you are, external situations will become as they are, automatically. Then you can communicate directly and accurately, not indulging in any kind of nonsense, any kind of emotional or philosophical or psychological interpretation. This third way is a balanced way of openness and communication which automatically allows tremendous space, room for creative development, space in which to dance and exchange.[1]

When we say "I love you" to a person, often we are hoping to lure them into our territory: "You must love me even if you hate me because I am intoxicated with love."

What does that mean? It means that I want the other person to let me have power over him; and the other person might easily reply, "If you really love me, how do I know that you won't create a claustrophobic situation with your heavy demands for love?" As long as I need security, as long as I make demands on other people, they will be suspicious of my "loving" attitude. Real caring is pure and fearless openness without conditions. There is no need to put on a pretty smile and play games. To be compassionate means to be adult.

> In the Buddhist teachings the symbol for compassion . . . is one moon shining in the sky while its image is reflected in one hundred bowls of water. The moon does not demand, "If you open to me, I will do you a favour and shine on you". The moon just shines. The point is not to want to benefit anyone or make them happy. There is no audience involved, no "me" and "them". It is a matter of an open gift, complete generosity without the relative notions of giving and receiving. That is the basic openness of compassion: opening without demand. Simply be what

you are, be the master of the situation. If you will just "be", then life flows around and through you.[2]

The ideal would be to

> "know and understand enough to be able to aid someone else in doing something necessary for himself, even when that person was not conscious of the need, and might work against you"; that only in this sense was love properly responsible and worthy of the name of real love . . . even with the best of intentions, most people would be too afraid to love another person in an active sense, or even to attempt to do anything for them; and that one of the terrifying aspects of love was that while it was possible to help another person to a certain degree, it was not possible to actually "do" anything for them. "If you see another man fall down, when he must walk, you can pick him up. But, although to take one more step is more necessary for him even than air, he must take this step alone; impossible for another person to take it for him."[3]

> Conscious love rarely obtains between humans; but it can be illustrated in the relations of man to his favourites in the animal and vegetable kingdoms. The development of the horse and the dog from their original state of nature; the cultivation of flowers and fruit – these are examples of a *primitive* form of conscious love, primitive because the motive is still egoistic and utilitarian. The conscious love motive, in its developed state, is the wish that the object should arrive at its own native perfection, regardless of the consequences of the lover. "So she become perfectly herself, what matter I?" says the conscious lover. "I will go to hell if only she may go to heaven." And the paradox of the attitude is that such love always evokes a similar attitude in its object. Conscious love begets conscious love.[4]

It is rare because most people want to be loved rather than to love, and rarely seek the perfecting of themselves or each other. They don't know what is the greatest good for those whom they love. In any case, conscious love only comes as a result of great inner effort and struggles on the part of a person who wishes to perfect himself in order one day to assist the perfecting of his beloved.

Love always creates. On the instinctive level it creates children, while on a higher level conscious love brings about the rebirth of the spirit.

> Everybody with perceptions beyond those of male and female must be aware of the change that comes over the man or woman, however old in years, who loves. It is usually instinctive; yet it symbolizes the still more marvellous change occurring when a man or woman loves consciously or is aware of being consciously loved. The youth in such cases has all the air of eternity; and it is, indeed, the divine youth. The creations of such a spiritual child in each of the two lovers is the peculiar function of conscious love: and it depends neither upon marriage nor upon children. There are other creations proper to still higher degrees of love; but they must remain until we have become as little children.[5]

"Take hold tightly, let go lightly." Sometimes the expression of love takes the form of letting go. This can be the hardest thing of all – there are so many reasons why it is difficult; one person may be afraid to let go because of an ideal of eternal fidelity, or because so much has been invested in a person, or because the circumstances are difficult in that both parties must go on seeing each other, or because one of the parties cannot bear the other to be happy without him or her.

> There are a thousand explanations, and every one of them, while sufficient as a cause, is quite inadequate as reason, the fact being that when one of the parties desires to

separate, the other's love-duty is to "let go". Great love can both let go and take hold.

Jealousy is the dragon in paradise; the hell of heaven; and the most bitter of the emotions because associated with the sweetest. There is a specific against jealousy, namely, conscious love; but this remedy is harder to find than the disease is to endure. But there are palliatives of which the first therapeutic condition is the recognition of the disease and the second the wish to cure oneself. In these circumstances let the sufferer deliberately experiment . . . he may plunge into new society. Or he may engage himself in a new work that demands all his energy. Or he may cast a spell on his memory and regard his former beloved as dead; or as having become his sister; or as having gone away on a long journey; or as having become enchanted. Best, however, if he "let go" completely with no lingering hope of ever meeting her again.

Be comforted. Our life is but one day of our Life. If not today, tomorrow! Let go![6]

Not every human being is capable of real love, but for a few love can be stronger than death. Viktor Frankl, a Jewish doctor and psychologist, was sent to a concentration camp during the last war. In all that he suffered the separation from his wife was one of the worst things that he had to endure. As he was stumbling on his way to work, urged on by a guard with a whip, and slipping on the ice, he looked up at the sky and saw the pink light of morning among the fading stars. He seemed to see his wife's face, her frank and encouraging look, which seemed to him brighter than the now rising sun. Then for the first time the truth struck him.

> *The salvation of man is through love and in love.* I understood how a man who has nothing left in this world still may know bliss, be it only for a brief moment, in the contemplation of his beloved. In a position of utter desolation, when man cannot express himself in positive action, when his only achievement may consist in enduring his sufferings in the right way – an honorable way – in such a position man can, through loving contemplation of the image he carries of his beloved, achieve fulfilment. For the first time in my life I was able to understand the meaning of the words, "The angels are lost in perpetual contemplation of an infinite glory".[7]

In front of him a man fell, and the guard used his whip on him. They reached the work site and began to hack at the frozen ground with pickaxes. Viktor Frankl realized that he did not know even whether his wife were still alive, but he knew that his love went far beyond the physical person of the beloved and found its deepest meaning in her inner spirit.

> There was no need for me to know; nothing could touch the strength of my love, my thoughts, and the image of my beloved. Had I known then that my wife was dead, I think that I would still have given myself, undisturbed by that knowledge, to the contemplation of her image, and that my mental conversation with her would have been just as vivid and just as satisfying. "Set me like a seal upon thy heart, love is as strong as death."[8]

It is good to strive to be worthy of love and to be loved. However, much as the love of another human being may be longed for, it is only a prefiguration of the one great Love, where we are known so intimately that every hair on our head is numbered, and yet are approached so delicately and sensitively that at any moment we have the freedom to say no or yes.

Love at a deeper level becomes more and more sensitive and vulnerable. Rumi, the Sufi mystic, said that we must become as sensitive and "trembling" as the new leaves on a tree. The leaves are the sensitive growing points of the tree; we must become the sensitive growing points of the world. I read somewhere that to be a saint is to be infinitely vulnerable.

> We have to make friends with ourselves completely, by developing what is known as *maitri*, or loving kindness, kindness to ourselves. Kindness to ourselves means kindness to whatever negativity arises and to whatever seems to be outside our discipline. We have to learn to relax and readmit chaos, which means having an open heart. This open heart is like a wound: it is tender, throbbing and alive. It brings the delightful discovery that fundamentally we are really quite soft. But when we look around, we see the whole world is struggling with that vulnerability and tenderness, trying to build steel, concrete and glass over the soft earth. So the mahayana path begins with maitri, the kindness that waters the soft earth so the seed of buddha nature can grow.[9]

As Rumi tells us, "A trembling and passionate heart is necessary in the search for God".

8

Forgiveness

I once hurt a friend of mine without meaning to; to my horror she ended the friendship. She refused to see me or answer the phone, and would not reply to my letters. It was terrible, not to be forgiven. For years I kept thinking that if only I could talk to her, if only she would let me explain, she would understand and forgive me, but it never happened.

Then someone whom I had gone out of my way to help, did me a great injury. For a long time when I thought of her a rage and hatred would grip me. These feelings went round and round in my head, endlessly.

One Sunday in church we were saying the "Our Father", when the words hit me with great force: "Forgive us our trespasses as we forgive those who trespass against us." She had trespassed against me, destroyed a part of my life, even. But did I want to be forgiven by God as I was forgiving her? I stopped and looked inside. I saw that there was no forgiveness there. There never could be. I would always go on hating her for what she had done. What did Christ's words mean then? I had to try to forgive. In desperation I prayed, and asked God to help me. I realized that I was never going to be able to forgive this person from myself, so I asked Him to forgive her in me. I saw that for this to happen I would have to make a space – my hatred had filled me completely. Every time the thought of her came up, I tried to make a space. To keep the space clear I could not indulge in revengeful thoughts or speak of her nastily.

Miraculously, it seemed to me, my hatred was taken away and I was given peace. From that peace I could wish her well.

It is very hard when one has been hurt, not to react.

Krishnamurti makes a distinction between a natural instinctive reaction, and a deliberate nursing of hatred:

> If someone sticks a pin into you, you are bound to react – protect yourself, or cry out in pain, or take yourself away from the offending agent – your reaction depending on several factors, varying from man to man. I mean hurt in the sense of nursing hatred. An event is over and for years we keep brooding over it, working ourselves up into a state of passion. The challenge of existence ever demands a fresh approach on our part to an issue or to an individual. A mind which nurses hatred, or for that matter nurses joy, long after the event is over, ceases to be sensitive . . .
>
> Let us say I am given to hating others. Now I must not go and start loving them, making love as a panacea for my foolish temperament. That way I shall never learn to grow out of my hateful nature. I will only be generating contradictions in myself, running from one conflict to another. What is wanted of me is to accept the fact that I hate others and then go into the cause of this. I should ask myself: why do I hate? Is it that I expect too much from life? Am I in any respect frustrated? What is it that I want? Am I capable enough to get it? I should ask myself all this, and stay in this state of exploration, without making any deliberate effort on my part to get rid of my malady. Suddenly I will discover that a transformation takes place in myself, without any planning on my part, a creative transformation. My sensitivity has now come into play![1]

Once my hatred had been taken away from me, and I was able to be more objective, I was able to see that in her circumstances I might have acted in the same way. I was no better than she, yet my own faults did not rouse in me the same rage!

> All evil qualities – oppression, hatred, envy, greed, mercilessness, pride – when they are within yourself, do not pain you. When you perceive them in another, then you

shy away and are pained. A man feels no disgust at his own scab and abscess; he will dip his affected hand into the broth and lick his fingers without turning in the least squeamish. But if he sees a tiny abscess or half a scratch on another's hand, he shies away from that man's broth and has no stomach for it whatever. Evil qualities are just like scabs and abscesses; when they are within a man himself he is not pained by them, but when he perceives them even to a small degree in another he is pained and disgusted.

Just as you shy away from your brother, so you should excuse him if he shies away from you and is pained. The pain you feel is his excuse, because your pain comes from perceiving those faults, and he perceives the same faults.[2]

It was hard to face up to my own faults, and yet I knew that this way offered the only possibility of developement.

Our unwillingess to see our own faults and the projection of them on to others is the source of most quarrels, and the strongest guarantee that injustice, animosity, and persecution will not easily die out.[3]

By seeing what is in myself, by seeing my own hatred and wounded vanity, forgiveness becomes possible because I see that the other person *is* me; whatever is in him or her is in me. Equally, if I cherish an evil emotion, I evoke the same back from others. Every thought has a consequence, good or bad.

Rolling Thunder, a medicine man working in America, warns about the dangers in the society around him.

If you have a sense of opposition – that is, if you feel contempt for others – you're in a perfect position to receive their contempt. The idea is not to be a receiver. You people have such anger and fear and contempt for your so-called criminals that your crime rate goes up and up. Your society has a high crime rate because it is in a perfect position to receive crime. You should be working *with* these people, not in opposition to them. The idea is to have contempt for crime, not for people. It's a mistake to think of any group or person as an opponent, because when you do, that's what the group or person will become. It's more useful to think of every other person as another *you* – to think of every individual as a representative of the universe.

Every person is plugged into the whole works. Nobody is outside it or affects it any less than anyone else. Every person is a model of life, so the true nature of a person is the nature of life. I don't care how low you fall or how high you climb, economically or academically or anything else, you still represent the whole thing. Even the worst criminal in life imprisonment sitting in his cell – the centre of him is the same seed, the seed of the whole creation.[4]

Difficult as it is to find forgiveness over a great injury, it is sometimes even harder to bear with and forgive the small annoying habits of those that we live with. Gurdjieff knew how hard this was:

> One of us asked: "Would it be a good task to bear the manifestations of others?"
>
> "To bear the displeasing manifestations of others is a big thing", he replied. "It is the last thing for a man. Only a man who has perfected himself can do this. Make it your aim to acquire the ability to bear one manifestation of one person that you now cannot endure without nervousness.
>
> "A useful exercise is to try to put oneself in another's place. For example, I know that A. is in a trying situation. He is dejected and morose. Half of him is trying to listen to me, the other half is occupied with his problem. I say

something to him that at another time would make him laugh, but now it makes him angry. But knowing him I shall try to put myself in his place and ask myself how I would respond.

"If I do this often enough I shall begin to see that if someone is bad-tempered there may be a reason for it which has nothing to do with me personally. We must try to remember that often it is not the person himself but his state that behaves irritably towards us. As I change, so does another."[5]

The one nearest you is always the one who gets on your nerves – no wonder that we are told to love our *neighbour*! The best description I have ever read of the struggle to love and forgive an annoying neighbour was by Hermann Hesse. He was staying in a hotel, and a noisy Dutchman moved in to the next room. Hesse was not able to change rooms and had to endure the noise of this man, his parties and racket far into the night. He could not write or sleep, and soon he began to hate this man with a violent, obsessional hatred. He began to imagine ways of killing him . . . Then one night he realized that he must overcome this feeling. He saw that his deepest belief had always been in the unity of all men – yet here he was, hating an innocent man. He set himself at that moment the task of loving his enemy. He saw that unless he could conquer his hate he was lost. With his writing and poetic skills, he set about trying to change the Dutchman from an object of hatred into an object of love, interest, sympathy and brotherhood. He began by imagining the Dutchman in front of him.

For the poet to love something means to catch it up in his imagination, to warm it and foster it there, to play with it, to saturate it with his own soul, to animate it with his own breath. This is what I did with my enemy until he belonged to me and had entered into me. Without his too-short neck I probably would not have succeeded, but his neck came to my rescue. . . . I could make him a soldier, a king, a beggar, a slave, an old man or a child, and in each one of these varied guises he had a short neck and slightly protuberant eyes. These characteristics were his weak points, they were where I must get hold of him. It was a long time before I succeeded in making the Dutchman grow younger, until I could see him before me as a young husband, as a bridegroom, as an undergraduate, as a schoolboy. When I had finally transformed him backwards into a small lad, that neck of his for the first time elicited my sympathy. By the gentle path of sympathy he won my heart when I saw this strong active boy causing his parents concern because of this slight indication of a tendency to asthma. By the gentle path of sympathy I proceeded to move forward in his life, and it took little art to envision the future years and stages. When I had got as far as seeing the whole man, older by ten years, suffering his first stroke, suddenly everything about him became touching, the thick lips, the heavy eyelids, the generally uninflected voice, everything enlisted my sympathy, and even before he had suffered death in my intense imagining, his mortality, his weaknesses, the necessity of his death, had come so close to me in brotherly feeling that I had long since lost all resistance to him. Then I was happy. I firmly closed his eyes and shut my own, for it was already morning and I was suspended like a ghost among the pillows, completely exhausted by my long night of poetical creation.

During the following day and night I had ample confirmation of the fact that I had conquered the Dutchman. The fellow could laugh or cough, he could sound as hearty as he liked, he could stride about noisily or push the chairs around or make jokes, but he no longer disturbed my equanimity. During the day I could work passably well, during the night I could rest passably well.

My triumph was great, but I did not enjoy it for long. On the second morning after my night of victory, the Dutchman suddenly left.

His place was taken by the perfect neighbour, a quiet old lady . . .

> For a number of days my new neighbour was a constant source of disillusionment. I would much rather have had my Dutchman back again, he whom I was now finally able to love.[6]

9
Suffering

My sister is a doctor, and she had helped to deliver many babies. Then she had her own first child. She told me afterwards that although when she was helping other mothers give birth, she had been very sympathetic about their pain, it was a very different matter when she was having the pain herself.

It is easy to philosophize about suffering; to undergo it is quite another matter. Suffering hurts. We all want to get away from it as quickly as we can. Unfortunately it is not always possible to get away, and then some means has to be found to cope with it.

We have inner resources that we do not know about until they are tapped. I remember the time when my eldest son had become ill. He was in a mental home, but he came home on visits, and during his visits I was under great stress, because I never knew when he was going to become hostile and violent. As he was bigger and stronger I was afraid of him. One day when he was particularly bad I went to a person I trusted and asked what I could do, because I was sick with fear. My friend advised me: "Don't try to do anything from yourself. If you do you are bound to fail. Instead, when you can find a time, go and sit quietly and ask for help from something inside yourself. I can promise that you will receive help." I did as he suggested, and it was as he said: I was given help at the moments when I needed it.

To bear suffering in the right way is an art. Even those who have undergone much suffering may miss the right way. The meaning of suffering is only revealed to the one who can accept and bear it. When a Zen priest fears that a sufferer under his care is not able to bear his suffering he will visit him often, not to relieve him, but to help him reach his inner self.

> He will try to make him face his suffering by bringing its full extent and magnitude to consciousness. He will help the sufferer to see that great suffering is not overcome by refusing to face it or by surrendering to it in despair. He will warn him of the danger of allowing himself to be solaced, and of waiting for time to heal. Salvation lies in giving full assent to his fate, serenely accepting what is laid upon him without asking why he should be singled out for so much suffering. Whoever is able to bear suffering in this way grows to the stature of his suffering, and he detaches himself from it by learning more and more to disregard the fact that it is *his* suffering.
>
> This detachment paves the way to healing, and healing follows of itself, the more sensitive he becomes to the suffering of others, and the more selflessly he shares their sufferings . . . The real meaning of suffering discloses itself only to him who has learned the art of compassion.[1]

If the sufferer has seen this clearly he will no longer try to run away from the suffering nor deny it. And if he shows that he is trying to accept his fate, then the priest will go on helping him. He will answer his questions, and will speak to him without preaching, but he will give something much more important than words.

> Gradually he will fall silent, and in the end will sit there wordless, for a long time, sunk deep in himself. And the strange thing is that this silence is not felt by the other person as indifference, as a desolate emptiness which disturbs rather than calms. It is as if this silence had more meaning than countless words could ever have. It is as if he were being drawn into a field of force from which fresh strength flows into him. He feels suffused with a strange confidence, even when his visitor has long since departed.

> And it may be that in these joyful hours, the resolve will be born to set out on the path that turns a wretched existence into a life of happiness.[2]

I wasn't always able to find that inner peace and support; sometimes I had to go on like a donkey, plodding with its head down.

One day in particular, I remember, I was at a very low ebb. My eldest son was attempting suicide every week, my younger son, in trying to help his brother, was becoming depressed himself. That morning I received a letter from my husband asking for a divorce. It seemed that I couldn't bear any more. I went to bed after lunch and covered up my head. Then I heard a knock at my bedroom door. It was Benny, my eldest son. He came into the room and sat down heavily on to a chair. "Have you ever been depressed, Mum?" he asked. "Well, yes, Benny, I have", I answered from under the blankets. "In fact I'm depressed now."

This was so unlike my usual forced cheerfulness with him that Benny was surprised. He stared at me without a word. I realized that somehow I had to keep going, even if it were only to the next hour. I said, "Benny, I read somewhere that if you help someone it makes you feel better, so why don't we try it? You go down and put the kettle on for me, and I'll then come down and make a cup of tea for you, and maybe we'll both feel better."

It must have worked because somehow we got through that terrible day.

Rolling Thunder, an Indian medicine man, thought that pain was a price we have to pay sometimes. Nothing comes free, everything has its cost.

> Every case of sickness and pain has its reason. And it's always a price that's being paid, either for something past or something future. But that doesn't mean we're not supposed to do something about sickness and pain. The important thing is to know how these things work. Modern

> doctors – most of them – don't seem to understand that. A medicine man's job is to look into these things. We know that everything is the result of something and the cause of something else, and it goes on like a chain. You can't just make the whole chain go away. Sometimes a certain sickness or pain is meant to be because it's the best possible price for something; you make that go away and the price becomes greater.
>
> I'm very interested in pain, and in relieving pain when it can be done by natural means. There are different spiritual conditions. Every physical thing in nature is a spiritual thing in spiritual nature. So these things can be spiritual helpers.[4]

It is possible that by accepting pain and suffering in the right way, we can pay for others, or pay in advance for ourselves.

When I had a long time of suffering from which I could not escape, I realized that I would have to accept it, and then I found that it could be transformed into spiritual energy.

There is a fairy tale about a girl who is locked into a tower and ordered on pain of death to spin straw into gold. A magic imp comes into the tower and promises to help her, on condition that she will belong to him unless she can find out his name. When the task is done, she names him, he disappears and she marries the King. This seemed to me a story with an inner meaning; suffering, like straw, can be transformed into gold, but for that it needs magic – help on another level – and even the devil can help me if I know him for what he is!

I tried to go on accepting the difficulties of my life, until my eldest son finally died, my divorce was over and my youngest son was no longer depressed, when I thought, "At last! Now I am going to be in for an easy time, nothing more can happen to me!"

At that point I started having trouble with my eyes. I went to an optician who sent me to a specialist, who told me that I would go blind in five years. To me, as an artist, this was worse than a sentence of death. I thought of all the long years ahead of me in darkness, and wondered "What have I got left?" I wanted to be angry with God but I couldn't – the habit of turning to Him in trouble was too great. Then I thought, "I am going to die anyway, maybe I can accept this as a first death to prepare me for the final death." Then I came across the writings of Jacques Lusseyran, a man who had been blinded as a boy of eight.

Lusseyran wrote that blindness had been his greatest happiness. What thirty-five years of blindness had taught him, he said, was to make great efforts. But more than efforts, they could be called discoveries.

> Barely ten days after the accident that blinded me, I made the basic discovery . . . I had completely lost the sight of my eyes: I could not see the light of the world any more. Yet the light was still there . . . I found it in myself, and what a miracle! – it was intact.
>
> This was something entirely new, you understand, all the more so since it contradicted everything that those who have eyes believe. The source of light is not the outer world. We believe that it is only because of a common delusion. The light dwells where life also dwells: within ourselves.
>
> Yet I had to make the effort to find my way between doors, walls, human beings, and trees. As happens to all blind persons, I hurt myself often. But I quickly learned that I knocked against things only when I forgot the light. When I paid constant attention to the light, I ran a much smaller risk.
>
> The second great discovery came almost immediately afterwards.

There was only one way to see the inner light, and that was to love.

> When I was overcome with sorrow, when I let anger take hold of me, when I envied those who saw, the light

> immediately decreased. Sometimes it even went out completely. Then I became blind. But this blindness was a state of not loving any more, of sadness; it was not the loss of one's eyes . . .
>
> However, courage, attention, joy, had the immediate effect of opening up and illuminating space . . . At the same time my physical adroitness increased; I found my way and moved with confidence . . .
>
> Blindness gives us great happiness. It gives us a great opportunity, both through its disorder and through the order it creates.
>
> The disorder is the prank it plays on us, the slight shift in causes. It forces us to see the world from another standpoint. This is a necessary disorder, because the principal reason for our unhappiness and our errors is that our standpoints are fixed.
>
> As for the order blindness creates, it is the discovery of the constantly present creation. We constantly accuse the conditions of our lives. We call them incidents, accidents, illnesses, duties, infirmities. We wish to force our own conditions on life; this is our real weakness. We forget that God never creates new conditions for us without giving us the strength to meet them. I am grateful that blindness has not allowed me to forget this.[5]

As I read this, it was as if a burden had been lifted from me. If this man could accept his blindness so completely, perhaps I could learn to do this too. I tried to stop worrying about my eyes, and they began to feel less strained.

My sister suggested that I see another specialist, and to my great joy, the original diagnosis was proved to be incorrect. I would be able to see!

Afterwards I realized that I had learned a great deal from that experience. For a little while I had been able to abandon myself to God and say, "Thy Will be done".

During that time of suffering, the great compensation was

that I felt God's presence very near, supporting me and enabling me to keep on from day to day. I remember a story told by a priest who had survived prison and torture in a communist country. He escaped and came to England where he was living comfortably. He said that now he often longed for the time in prison, because in spite of the terrible conditions and pain he had suffered then, he had felt such a closeness to God.

It seems that with His help we can endure all things . . .

> God does not entirely heal those who have broken hearts. He only eases their suffering, lest it torment and deject them. For dejection is not good and not pleasing to God. A broken heart prepares man for the service of God, but dejection corrodes service. We must distinguish between the two as carefully as between joy and wantonness; they are so easily confused, and yet are as far removed from one another as the ends of the earth.
>
> We do not even know how we are supposed to pray. All we do is call for help because of the need of the moment. But what the soul intends is spiritual need, only we are not able to express what the soul means. That is why we do not merely ask God to hear our call for help, but also beg him, who knows what is hidden, to hear the silent cry of the soul.[6]

Different ways of dealing with suffering help at different times. Viktor Frankl (the doctor I have quoted earlier in connection with love) was at a very low ebb in a concentration camp – he was starving and cold, with terrible pain from sores on his feet. He made a great effort of will to think of another subject.

Suddenly he saw himself on a platform in a warm, well-lit room. An audience in comfortable chairs was listening to him lecturing on the psychology of people in the concentration camp.

To his surprise he was able to rise above the sufferings of that moment and view his troubles as if they were already in the past. He himself had become the object of an interesting psychological study undertaken by himself. He quotes a saying of Spinoza: "Emotion, which is suffering, ceases to be suffering as soon as we form a clear and precise picture of it."

Later on, there came a particularly bad day to the men in the camp. As a punishment for one prisoner's misdemeanour, they were all made to fast for a day. That evening as they lay in their earthen huts, the lights suddenly went out. Tempers reached a very low ebb. Then the senior block warden asked Viktor Frankl to talk to the men, so that they did not give up hope completely. He himself was cold and hungry, but he did not want to fail his comrades. He spoke first about the possibility of the Allies winning, in which case, as they each had their skills, they could win back all that they had lost. They still had their bones intact, and as Nietzsche said, "What doesn't kill me, makes me stronger". He went on to say that although he himself estimated his chances of survival as only about one in twenty, he had no intention of losing hope or giving up while there was still a chance. It was the ones who gave up hope who died soonest.

He told them that all that they had experienced in the past was not for nothing. They had brought it into being, and no one could take that away from them.

He spoke about giving a meaning to life.

> I told my comrades (who lay motionless, although occasionally a sigh could be heard) that human life, under any circumstances, never ceases to have a meaning, and that this infinite meaning of life includes suffering and dying, privation and death. I asked the poor creatures who listened to me attentively in the darkness of the hut to face up to the seriousness of our position. They must not lose

hope but should keep their courage in the certainty that the hopelessness of our struggle did not detract from its dignity and its meaning. I said that someone looks down on each of us in difficult hours – a friend, a wife, somebody alive or dead, or a God – and he would not expect us to disappoint him. He would hope to find us suffering proudly – not miserably – knowing how to die.

And finally I spoke of our sacrifice, which had meaning in every case.

Those of us who had any religious faith, I said frankly, could understand without difficulty. I told them of a comrade who on his arrival in camp had tried to make a pact with Heaven that his suffering and death should save the human being he loved from a painful end. For this man suffering and death were meaningful; his was a sacrifice of the deepest significance. He did not want to die for nothing. None of us wanted that.

The purpose of my words was to find a full meaning in our life, then and there, in that hut and in that practically hopeless situation. I saw that my efforts had been successful. When the electric bulb flared up again, I saw the miserable figures of my friends limping toward me to thank me with tears in their eyes.[7]

10

In Search of Happiness

After I had been through so many years of suffering, my life became peaceful again. At first this tranquillity was enough for me, but then I began to feel that I was missing something. I was entitled to happiness. Various longings took hold of me; I would achieve worldwide fame as an artist, I would become fabulously rich; above all, now that I was living on my own, I dreamed of the perfect man who would come into my life; we would marry, and live happily ever after.

With this dream in view I embarked on several relationships, but they all ended unhappily. For a few moments of happiness I paid with months of heart-ache, and the more I longed for such a relationship the further away it seemed to recede, while my craving grew stronger.

> Sensation is one thing, and happiness is another. Sensation is always seeking further sensation, ever in wider and wider circles. There is no end to the pleasures of sensation; they multiply, but there is always dissatisfaction in their fulfilment; there is always the desire for more, and the demand for more is without end. Sensation and dissatisfaction are inseparable, for the desire for more binds them together . . . In the very act of the fulfilment of sensation, the demand for more is born. The more is ever in the future . . . Physical sensations are always crying for more; and when they are thwarted, there is anger, jealousy, hatred.[1]

There is a story of a dervish who stopped a king in the street and challenged him to fill his begging bowl. The King ordered it to be filled with gold, but to his astonishment as fast as he filled it with gold coins, it emptied. Sack after sack was brought and still the bowl could not be filled.

> "Stop!" shouted the King, "for this trickster is emptying my treasury!"
>
> "To you I am emptying your treasury," said the dervish, "but to others I am merely illustrating a truth."
>
> "And the truth?" asked the King.
>
> "The truth is that, the bowl is the desires of man, and the gold what man is given. There is no end to man's capacity to devour, without being in any way changed."[2]

There was a gnawing desperate hunger in me that went through every area of my life, craving for love, for excitement, for food. I kept wanting to rush through the moment that I was in, so that I could get on with the next moment. I even caught myself hurrying through chewing one bite of a biscuit in order to rush into the next bite!

What was driving me like this so that I could never relax and enjoy the moment? Was it my desire for happiness? I asked myself one day, "When do I actually *experience* happiness?" I made two lists:

What I imagine will make me happy	*What brings me the experience of happiness*
Parties	Painting
Travel	Writing
New clothes	Walking in the country
Romance	Talking with friends

Here I stopped and asked myself what the difference between the lists was. It occured to me then that the happiness in the first list was all in the future; I liked the idea of travel because I dreamed of getting somewhere interesting. I hankered after new clothes because I dreamed of being admired in them;

parties, because I dreamed of romance; romance, because I dreamed of getting married again.

The occasions on which I was really happy were not so glamorous. They even involved a certain effort on my part. But they were concerned with here and now, I didn't need to dream about them and – miracle! – they were available to me right now!

So why wasn't I happy? Was it because my desires were getting in the way?

> There is no crime greater than having too many desires;
> There is no disaster greater than not being content;
> There is no misfortune greater than being covetous.
> Hence in being content, one will always have enough.[3]

It depressed me that I was such a bundle of desires, but then I read that one can harness the force that goes into desiring something. Gurdjieff often spoke about the necessity of struggle if we want to reach a higher level in ourselves. One suggestion he made to a pupil was that she try giving up smoking for a while, and turn her longing for a cigarette into a contact with a higher world. He said that her struggle would be not to buy the cigarette, to break this habit, outwardly, and also her inner struggle with the longing, when her imagination pictures how it was when she used to smoke, but pictures it more keenly, with more longing.

> This can be a thing for power. I will tell you one very important thing to say, each time when the longing to smoke comes. You say it the first time, and maybe notice nothing. You say it a second time, and maybe nothing. Say it a third time, and perhaps something will happen. Say: "I wish the result of this suffering to become my own, for Being." Yes, you can call that kind of wishing suffering, because it *is* suffering.
>
> This saying can maybe *take force from your animal* and give it to Being. And you can do this for many things – for any

> denial of something that is a *slavery*. A force such as this has special results, special emanations.
>
> Man is man – he can never be another thing. But he can make his body work for another part of him – his mind. If it is easy to subdue the body, then the exercise is no good. If the body will lie down at once, nothing happens. The greater weakness the body has, the more it is forced to struggle, the more labour it does, the more it can give to the mind, and to Being.[4]

> If a man gives way to all his desires, or panders to them, there will be no inner struggle in him, no "friction", no fire. But if, for the sake of attaining a definite aim, he struggles with desires that hinder him, he will then create a fire which will gradually transform his inner world into a single whole.[5]

I found that I felt better when I tried to do battle with my desires. The struggle brought me something real which the thing I had desired rarely did; and often the thing desired turned out to have been an illusion anyway. In the past I have impatiently waited for a Thursday and Friday to pass quickly because of a party on Saturday; but when I was at the party it would be a disappointment, while the days that I had pushed aside so impatiently might turn out on retrospect to be the ones that I remembered and cherished. I came to see that it was a waste of time looking forward to things too much because you could never tell – the longed-for event often proved to be a fiasco, while something I dreaded might turn out to be a marvellous experience.

Bearing this in mind, I began to try to curb my headlong rush towards the next event that promised happiness, and in doing this I began to slow down and take notice of intervals. Intervals were sections of time that I had previously disregarded and thrown away. They were times spent waiting at bus stops, train stations or airports; in the dentist's waiting room or the doctor's surgery.

I could use that time instead of throwing it away. I began to plan my intervals, I took books and writing materials with me whenever I went out. (I am writing this now waiting at a station for a delayed train.) Of course, it is not always possible to write or even read in every situation when one is delayed – for example while waiting in a queue at the supermarket. But there is always one thing that it is possible to do, the most profitable thing of all. Prayer is always possible. In a twinkling of an eye I can be lifted out of my impatience, my greed, my unhappiness. Little by little all my intervals begin to add up and join together. Instead of being pulled by impatient longing, something in me becomes more tranquil.

I began to see that my chasing after happiness was a way of trying to escape the suffering that life inevitably brings. Whether married or single, life consists of the same material for everyone. It is funny, boring, interesting and unsatisfying. No other human being could deliver me from the stuff of which life is composed. But I could begin to try to deliver myself. What I could search for instead was something that had been there inside me all the time, waiting patiently until I stopped running outwards long enough to notice it: that peace which no man can take from you.

> So it is with all desires and affections, all loves and fondnesses which people have for every variety of thing – father, mother, heaven, earth, gardens, palaces, branches of knowledge, acts, things to eat and drink. The man of God realizes that all these desires are the desire for God, and all those things are veils. When men pass out of this world and behold that King without these veils, then they will realize that all those were veils and coverings, their quest being in reality that One Thing. All difficulties will then be resolved, and they will hear in their hearts the answer to all questions and all problems, and every thing will be seen face to face.[6]

Whatever happiness is in the world
Has all arisen from a wish for the
Welfare of other beings.

Whatever misery there is has arisen
From indulging in selfishness.[7]

And joy is everywhere; it is in the earth's green coverage of grass; in the blue serenity of the sky; in the reckless exuberance of spring; in the severe abstinence of grey winter; in the living flesh that animates our bodily frame; in the perfect poise of the human figure, noble and upright; in living; in the exercise of all our powers; in the acquisition of knowledge; in fighting evils; in dying for gains we never can share. Joy is there everywhere; it is superfluous, unnecessary; nay, it very often contradicts the most peremptory behests of necessity. It exists to show that the bonds of law can only be explained by love; they are like body and soul. Joy is the realization of the truth of oneness, the oneness of our soul with the world and of the world-soul with the supreme lover.[8]

The clouds above us join and separate.
The breeze in the courtyard leaves and
Returns
Life is like that, so why not
Relax?
Who can stop us from celebrating?[9]

11

Fear and Freedom

I was a very frightened child. When I wasn't worrying about meeting the school bully on the playground, I was torturing myself with fears of illness and death. I was convinced that I would get leprosy. My older sister had given me a graphic account of it: "First your finger drops off, then your toes drop off, and then everything else drops off and you're dead." She would also frighten me by asking what I would do if I were commanded to give up my faith or be tortured to death. In spite of my protestations I knew deep down that I would agree to anything rather than be hurt. I could not overcome any of my imaginary fears.

Later I found that real problems can be accepted and coped with. This is because in real things God is there to help. He is not there in imagined problems.

> Go forward then, without fear. Forsake childish things and, above all, take courage; for a hundred vicissitudes will come upon you unawares.[1]

> "I'll have you hanged," said a cruel and ignorant king, who had heard of Nasrudin's powers, "if you don't prove that you are a mystic."
>
> "I see strange things," said Nasrudin at once; "a golden bird in the sky, demons under the earth."
>
> "How can you see through solid objects? How can you see far into the sky?"
>
> "Fear is all you need."[2]

Irmis Popoff, a pupil of Ouspensky in New York, found it a great relief when she was able to see clearly that most people are afraid of each other, and so were all putting on an act. While she was putting on an act to impress them, they were putting on an act to impress her! In seeing this she began to be more free.

> Little by little I was freed from other people in this sense. I understood, by the taste of it, that I was responsible only to myself and no one else, because others were not at all sure of themselves either. Surface criticism, rebuff, harshness, disdain – all equally superficial. One can upset them with a simple glance at so innocuous a thing as a person's shoelace. A glance in the direction of anything equally idiotic will turn over many an apple cart!
>
> Many years later, as a result of diligent work in this direction, I came to feel that I was responsible to myself, and myself alone, for anything I felt, thought, wore, said, or did. I was not running in a contest or competing with anyone for admiration or acceptance; rebuke and applause were equally useless to me, because it was I alone who had to accept or reject myself. With this realization I began to shed my fetters.[3]

We moved to a small neighbourhood community when my three boys were very small, and there a large Italian family continually asked me to babysit for them. I was so anxious to appear obliging that I was afraid to say no, but after a while I began to hate them. At last I went to my parish priest and confessed in tears that I hated this family! When I told him the whole story he said, "Can't you tell them that you don't like doing this?" I was amazed at this simple solution.

"You placate people too much", he told me. "Is that bad for me?" I asked.

"It's bad for them", he answered, and went on with a smile, "I used to placate people too, then when I saw that I was doing this I decided to stop. But it was difficult to begin with people I knew so I tried it out first by being very curt on buses and in shops." He had made me reflect a great deal. I saw that I was a slave to other people's opinion of me. On the next occasion that the family asked me to babysit I was able to say no, and my hatred disappeared.

> . . . thought creates fear. And fear cannot end through the mere control or suppression of thought, or by trying to transmute thought, or indulging in all the tricks one plays on oneself. Realizing this whole pattern choicelessly, objectively, in oneself, seeing all this, thought itself says, "I will be quiet without any control or suppression", "I will be still".
>
> So then there is the ending of fear, which means the ending of sorrow and the understanding of oneself – self-knowing. Without knowing oneself there is no ending of sorrow and fear. It is only a mind that is free from fear that can face reality.[4]

With regard to the imaginary fears, I was greatly helped by Dr Maurice Nicoll. He wrote in his *Psychological Commentaries* that, when riding on the top of a double-decker bus, he used to have a terrible fear that it would fall over. One day he got the idea of "willing" it to fall over, and his fear disappeared.

Dr Viktor Frankl (quoted earlier in the chapters on Love and Suffering) used this strange fact in his therapy with his patients. He wrote:

> Ironically enough, in the same way that fear brings to pass what one is afraid of, a forced intention makes impossible what one forcibly wishes.[5]

That is, if a patient were afraid of something, he was recommended to will that very thing, and that made his fear disappear.

Dr Frankl gives several examples of this effect. In one a young physician came to him because of his fear of perspiring. Since he was so afraid of it, the anxiety was bringing on even greater sweating. Dr Frankl advised the patient that, when next he feared an attack of sweating, he should decide deliberately that he would show people how much he could sweat.

A week later the young physician returned, saying that whenever anyone had triggered off his fear of perspiring, he had said to himself:

> "I only sweated out a quart before, but now I'm going to pour at least ten quarts!" The result was that, after suffering from his phobia for four years, he was able, after a single session, to free himself permanently of it within one week.[6]

A man who has struggled with his fears can eventually become more free from them. Then when there is a crisis, only such a man is free to make a choice. For example, if a fire breaks out most people in their panic and fear become slaves to their instinct to preserve their life at all costs, but the man who is more free can make a conscious choice to help someone else, even at risk to himself.

When I was in Kamakura, in Japan, I spoke with a Zen master who told us about a pupil of his who was in an aeroplane which was threatened by terrorists. She wrote that she had tried to recollect herself at that moment, and had been able to help others keep calm. When it was over everyone had wanted to know how she could maintain her presence of mind at such a time. She seemed, they said, completely free from fear.

> Choice of action is possibly only if a man is free inside. An ordinary man cannot choose, he cannot form a critical estimate of the situation; with him, his external is his internal. It is necessary to learn to be unbiased, to sort out and analyze each action as though one were a stranger. Then one can be just. To be just at the very moment of action is a hundred times more valuable than to be just afterwards. A great deal is necessary for this. An unbiased attitude is the basis of inner freedom, the first step toward free will.[7]

> If a man places a gulf between himself and God, this gulf will bring fear. But if a man finds the support of the Invisible and Ineffable, he is free from fear.[8]

Dr Frankl writes of people being able to keep their freedom of mind even under the worst conditions, in the concentration camps:

> We who lived in concentration camps can remember the men who walked through the huts comforting others, giving away their last piece of bread. They may have been few in number, but they offer sufficient proof that everything can be taken from a man but one thing: the last of the human freedoms – to choose one's attitude in any given set of circumstances, to choose one's own way.[9]

It seems that even at the worst moments physically, there was nevertheless a possibility for the prisoner to choose what kind of person he would become, to decide what he would be, mentally and spiritually.

> He may retain his human dignity even in a concentration camp. Dostoevski said once, "There is only one thing that I dread: not to be worthy of my sufferings." These words frequently came to my mind after I became acquainted with those martyrs whose behaviour in camp, whose suffering and death, bore witness to the fact that the last inner freedom cannot be lost. It can be said that they were worthy of their sufferings; the way they bore their suffering was a genuine inner achievement. It is this spiritual freedom – which cannot be taken away – that makes life meaningful and purposeful.[10]

Viktor Frankl goes on to tell of the moment of release for the prisoners in the concentration camp. Having lived so long a life of fear and deprivation, they didn't know how to deal with their new freedom. They could not grasp it, however often they repeated to themselves the word "Freedom".

When they went out of the camp, something they had longed for so much before, they looked at the outside world with listless eyes. They saw flowers and meadows but they could not feel anything about them. They had all lost the ability to feel pleased, and had to relearn it again. Everything felt like a dream to them. So often in the past they had dreamed that they were free, only to be woken by the shrill whistle of the guards. Now that freedom had really come, they could not at first receive it.

> One day, a few days after the liberation, I walked through the country past flowering meadows, for miles and miles, toward the market town near the camp. Larks rose to the sky and I could hear their joyous song. There was no one to be seen for miles around; there was nothing but the wide earth and sky and the larks' jubilation and the freedom of space. I stopped, looked around, and up to the sky – and then I went down on my knees. At that moment there was very little I knew of myself or of the world – I had but one sentence in mind – always the same: "I called to the Lord from my narrow prison and He answered me in the freedom of space."
>
> How long I knelt there and repeated this sentence memory can no longer recall. But I know that on that day, in that hour, my new life started. Step for step I progressed, until I again became a human being.
>
> The crowning experience of all, for the homecoming man, is the wonderful feeling that, after all he has suffered, there is nothing he need fear any more – except his God.[11]

12

Pride

My son Desmond, when he was small, liked to tell everyone about his successes in schoolwork and sport. One day he was accused of boasting. He was very worried by this, and puzzled.

"But if you don't tell people that you come first," he protested, "how are they to know?"

I knew how he felt. When I was a young girl I had become used to a lot of praise because I was able to draw well. Then a nun in the convent school that I went to, said "It is not *your* gift, it was given by God", and I didn't like to hear that, it seemed to take away from my own glory.

But after many years I began to be a little tired of my self-glorification. It seemed as if people had only to press a button by praising me, and something in me would pop out like a monkey and begin prancing around in feathers and sequins. Seeing this monkey in myself helped me in my struggle against vanity.

Seeing pride was harder. I noticed it in other people first. They'd say things like "I have dropped my ego a long time ago" and "In spite of my success I have absolutely no vanity". Then a little warning bell would sound in my ear. I began to hear myself saying the same kind of thing, "Now that I recognize my vanity it has no power over me any more".

My pride wouldn't die. Even at my most humble moments, I detected a pride in actually being humble.

> Then came the sparrow of feeble body and tender heart, trembling like a flame. She said, "I am frail as a hair. I have no one to help me, and I have not the strength of an ant. I

> have neither down nor feathers – nothing. How can a weakling like me make her way to the Simurgh?". . . .
>
> The hoopoe replied: "O you who are sometimes sad, sometimes gay, I am not deceived by these artful pleas. You are a little hypocrite. Even in your humility you show a hundred signs of vanity and pride."[1]

Pride expresses itself in little things as well as big: sometimes the worst thing, the most damaging to other people, is an unspoken assumption of superiority. Colonists do that to the people in the colonies. I do that to people I meet at bus-stops, or group meetings. I was taught a lesson one day at a conference. We were all seated round a table, having a discussion. There were many eminent men there, myself, and what seemed a very ordinary-looking elderly woman, whom nobody allowed to say much. A conversation began about Gandhi, and I was anxious to put in my contribution, as I had been to India and was very interested in him. The older woman opened her mouth to say something, but nobody allowed her to speak. I thought patronizingly, "It would be charitable at least to let her have her say" and asked her to speak. It transpired that she herself had worked with Gandhi for many years in India, and could tell us marvellous stories about him. I never made snap judgements about people again, after that!

I began to see that all pride is hypocrisy, or leads to it. This is because pride is basically a lie. It is pretending that I am what I am not: that my gifts come from myself, that my life comes from myself, that of myself I am not only worth a great deal, but that I am worth more than other people.

To see the truth of what I am takes courage. I must give up my illusions about what I am and try to catch myself unawares.

> Perhaps it is not possible to define vanity except by examples; we can see its manifestations in others, but to see them in ourselves – at the time, and not afterwards – is almost impossible. In times of mass psychosis these two enemies, vanity and self-love, are intensified. On one

occasion in the war the commanding officer of my battalion sacrificed, from vanity, the lives of twenty men rather than admit that he was wrong.[2]

Seeing oneself may be difficult and painful, but it is our only hope. The worst thing is to pretend to myself that I am "good".

Often we think what we have done is good, but it may not actually be so. When we become old, we are often very proud of what we have done. When others listen to someone proudly telling something which he has done, they will feel funny, because they know his recollection is one-sided. They know that what he has told them is not exactly what he did. Moreover, if he is proud of what he did, that pride will create some problem for him. Repeating his recollections in this way, his personality will be twisted more and more, until he becomes quite a disagreeable, stubborn fellow. This is an example of leaving a trace of one's thinking. We should not forget what we did, but it should be without an extra trace . . . What we call "attachment" is just these traces of our thought and activity . . . the important thing is self-reflection. There is nothing I can do about cases of satisfaction without self-reflection, or of compliance without self-reformation.[3]

It is hard to stop being a hypocrite. The moment I think I have achieved something worthwhile I start thinking that I must be rather special, better than other people, in fact. From then on I bracket myself in a separate place, and I also bracket others. In fact I begin to put them in separate boxes and myself in a special box, an ivory-tower-like box. Now I am unassailable – but on the other hand I can't receive anything either.

Only a life lived in a certain spirit is worth living. It is a remarkable fact that a life lived entirely from the ego is dull not only for the person himself but for all concerned.[4]

Although it is very difficult, it is also a great relief to step down out of the box and be on the same earth as other people. When I am trying to get them to admit my superiority, then every person is a threat to me, but if I am wishing to know the truth, then every man is my friend and helper.

C. S. Nott remembers Gurdjieff speaking on the subject:

> Merslukin called me a fool. But why should I feel hurt? . . . I think about it, I reason about it. I say to myself: "If he called me a fool, does it follow that he is wise? Perhaps he is a fool himself. He acts like a child, and you cannot expect children to be wise. Perhaps someone has been talking to him about me and he has got foolish ideas. So much the worse for him. . . .
>
> "On the other hand I may have been a fool. In this case I should thank him for letting me see that I have behaved like a fool. In neither case am I hurt."[5]

Although it is discouraging to see one's faults, it is the only way of becoming more free from pride.

Margaret Anderson recounts an incident which occurred in Paris while she was a pupil of Gurdjieff:

> "Past joys", he said, "are as useless to man in the present as the snows of last year which leave no trace by which one can remember what they were. Only the imprints of conscious labour and intentional suffering are Real, and can be used for obtaining good."
>
> This good comes to you step by step, in great "discoveries" – for instance, like the one that teaches you why anger is so often an expression of self-love. I shall never forget the day when I first "learned" this truth. I had spent a week of frenzied anger and rebellion over everything Gurdjieff was asking me to do. The conscious labour was too difficult, the voluntary suffering too unendurable, too impossible, too unreasonable. And then, in one lighted moment, I had a picture of myself, my state, and its cause.

I rushed to the rue des Colonels Renard and said, "Mr Gurdjieff, I see now that it was because of my vanity and self-love that I was so angry."

He didn't speak for a moment, then he smiled at me. "You not know?" he said.

"No," I said, "I hadn't the faintest idea."

Never, never, shall I forget the way he smiled, or the intonation he put into those three words. Never shall I fail to remember them as I watch myself making other discoveries that will take me as long a time; and never shall I fail to find comfort in six other words of his: "He who goes slow goes far."[6]

It is because of this danger that we should be pleased when anything humbles us.

In our scriptures (Samyuktagama Sutra, volume 33), it is said that there are four kinds of horses: excellent ones, good ones, poor ones, and bad ones. The best horse will run slow and fast, right and left, at the driver's will, before it sees the shadow of the whip; the second best will run as well as the first one does, just before the whip reaches its skin; the third one will run when it feels pain on its body; the fourth will run after the pain penetrates to the marrow of its bones. You can imagine how difficult it is for the fourth one to learn how to run!

When we hear this story, almost all of us want to be the best horse . . . If you think the aim of Zen practice is to train you to become one of the best horses, you will have a big problem. This is not the right understanding. If you practise Zen in the right way it does not matter whether you are the best horse or the worst one. When you consider the mercy of Buddha, how do you think Buddha will feel about the four kinds of horses? He will have more sympathy for the worst one than for the best one.

When you are determined to practise zazen with the great mind of Buddha, you will find the worst horse is the most valuable one. In your very imperfections you will find the basis for your firm way-seeking mind . . . So I think that sometimes the best horse may be the worst horse, and the worst horse can be the best one.[7]

When I read this piece by Suzuki, I thought of the quotation in the Bible: "The first shall be last and the last shall be first."

A man of piety complained to the Baalshem, saying: "I have laboured hard and long in the service of the Lord, and yet I have received no improvement. I am still an ordinary and ignorant person."

The Baalshem answered: "You have gained the realization that you are ordinary and ignorant, and this in itself is a worthy accomplishment."[8]

Here there is a paradox, for it is also important to value oneself in the right way. There is something in each person that is of infinite value. As C. S. Lewis said, "The important thing is not to say 'I'm not special' but 'Everyone is as special as I am'".

Everyone must have two pockets, so that he can reach into the one or the other, according to his needs. In his right pocket are to be the words: "For my sake was the world created", and in his left: "I am earth and ashes."[9]

Pride being the deadliest of the deadly sins, we should be thankful to help ourselves get rid of it by any means. But the very words "get rid of" are a mistake. In a sense we never can rid ourselves of pride, because the more we ascend in spiritual levels the more we can be tempted by spiritual pride.

I remember once when I was in Paris, I visited Notre Dame Cathedral. There I saw on the lower levels gargoyles representing the different vices of man. As one went up higher the gargoyles seemed to become more abstract – to represent pure hatred or greed or lust. High above them soared the spires, seeming at last to have rid themselves of all vices, except one. For leaping out from the great heights were the cold serpents of pride.

> If your practice is good, you may become proud of it. What you do is good, but something more is added to it. Pride is extra. Right effort is to get rid of something extra.[10]

> Admiration of oneself is among the most powerful mystical faults which can pervert the soul of the worshipper, even if he has arrived at the spiritual level called the "diamond", where the lights of the hidden name appear in colourless rays.[11]

Martin Buber says that pride is so dangerous for us that it would be better to be a bad man than a proud one.

> There are two extremes among men. One sort of man is wholly evil. He knows his Lord, yet deliberately defies him. The other thinks he is wholly righteous, and people take him at his own value. But though he studies and prays incessantly and mortifies his flesh, he toils in vain, for he has no true faith. And this is the difference between them: he who is all evil can be cured of his infirmity when he wakens to the Turning, and turns to God with a whole heart and begs him to point the way to the light. But that other, who has not the possibility of recognizing the greatness of his Creator and the true nature of service because, in his own eyes, he is righteous – how can he turn?
>
> There is no room for God in him who is full of himself.[12]

In our catechism it used to say that pride was the sin against the Holy Spirit for which there was no forgiveness. I often used to wonder about that until I realized that another word for forgive is to "cancel". But pride leads to a lack of growth. When I think I am sufficient to myself, I stop turning to God for nourishment – and I stop growing. No forgiveness can cancel out my lack of growth; although the moment that I turn towards God again, in seeing what I really am, the pride drops for a moment, then I am able to grow again.

It is God who makes me grow, or who grows in me, but to do that he needs my consent, my willingess to say at any moment, "Not I that live but Thou that livest in me".

> It is infinitely difficult to renounce even a very slight pleasure or to expose oneself to a very slight pain solely for the sake of God, the true God, that is to say, the one who is in heaven and not anywhere else. Because to make that effort is an approach, not towards suffering but towards death; and towards a death which is more radical than that of the body and equally repellent to nature: the death of the thing within us that says "I".[13]

13

Letting Go

When I was a little girl I used to collect pieces of broken glass, calling them my "jewels". I hoarded beads, feathers, and lace, and made ornaments for my dolls with them. My older sister and I had fierce tussles over our possessions.

One day my sister suddenly gave me all her treasures. It was the first intimation of the spiritual vocation that she was to follow. I was dumbfounded. Now that the possessions could no longer be fought over, they had lost half their lustre.

When I was in my twenties I did the same thing; I gave away all the things that were most precious to me: my art books and jewellery. I wanted my husband to regain his faith in God, but the sacrifice did not work. Yet it is possible that no sacrifice is ever made in vain. I did receive something from this gesture: from then on, possessions lost their hold over me.

Instead I began to put all my value on to people: my family and friends. Like Polonius, I wanted to "bind them to my soul with hoops of steel". But like a mirage, the more I rushed forward to grasp affection, the more it receded. My friends had their separate lives to lead, my marriage ended in divorce, my children began to grow up and prepare to leave home, my eldest son died.

I saw that I must put my treasure on higher things, so I aimed now at spiritual advancement. I made enormous efforts, visualizing myself as a great saint one day. However, with all my efforts I still caught myself out in moments of anger, irritation, or greed. It was very disheartening!

> *"It is when your practice is rather greedy that you become discouraged with it. So you should be grateful that you have a*

sign or warning signal to show you the weak point in your practice."

There are several poor ways of practice which you should understand. Usually when you practise zazen, you become very idealistic, and you set up an ideal or goal which you strive to attain and fulfil. But as I have often said, this is absurd. When you are idealistic, you have some gaining idea within yourself; by the time you attain your ideal or goal, your gaining idea will create another ideal. So as long as your practice is based on a gaining idea, and you practise zazen in an idealistic way, you will have no time actually to attain your ideal.[1]

At last I began to see that I was grasping after spiritual attainment as greedily as I gobbled chocolates as a child. The fact that this time my greed was directed at things of the spirit did not change the nature of the thing that drove me. It was still greed.

There is a story from the time of Buddha about a beggar woman who was very poor. She wanted so much, and this made her feel even more poor. She decided to follow Buddha, who was at a feast, and in this way she hoped to beg some food from him. He saw her standing near him and asked her what she wanted. She begged him greedily for some food. He said:

"In that case you must first say No. You have to refuse when I offer it to you." He held out the food to her, but she found it very difficult to say No. She realized that in all her life she had never said No. Whenever anyone had anything or offered her anything she had always said, "Yes, I want it". So she found it very difficult to say No, as she was not at all familiar with that word. After great difficulty she finally did say No and then Budha gave her the food. And through this she realized that the real hunger inside her was the desire to own, grasp, possess and want.[2]

> If you are terribly hungry and thirsty, you want to attack the universe as your prey all at once: "I'll have it for my dinner or my breakfast. I don't care." You don't think about anybody else who might have just a humble request, who might just want to have a sip from your glass of milk or a piece of meat from your plate. If you are told that you should be devotional, you might think that means that you should be even more hungry and try to get every possible blessing into your system. Since you are hungry, you suck up everything, all the systems and resources that exist, including your own. You don't find yourself being a productive human being; instead you find yourself becoming a monster.[3]

I began to see that you can't approach the spiritual level in that grasping spirit. Any virtues obtained in that state of mind would just go towards feeding my vanity.

There is a story about a woman who had been following a guru for years, pestering him to give her enlightenment. She wanted to hear mystical voices, use divining cards and undergo mysterious rituals. At last the guru realized that although she had become very subdued, she was only biding her time, and would soon again demand secrets and mysteries instead of real teaching. He decided on a final interview:

> "Here at last are your instructions", he said. "You will drink some holy water, fast for three months and repeat this word ninety million times. Then you will walk to Katmandu, measuring your length along the way, never lose your temper, strain every fibre to hear celestial music, and never say a metaphysical word. Then you will stop doing all these things and go back to ordinary life as you know it!"
>
> "O Master!" she breathed; "and will I then be in a state of perfect freedom and release?"
>
> "No, but you'll feel as if you were!"[4]

I began to see that as long as I still wanted something from the spiritual world, I was on the wrong track. Trungpa tells us that if we are looking for miracles and liberation, then we are bound by the "golden chain of spirituality". This chain may be beautiful to wear, but it imprisons us. People who think that they can use spirituality for personal adornment are deceiving themselves. Instead of magical powers, we have to face the ordinary task of working on ourselves, and our suffering.

We have to allow ourselves to be disappointed, and give up all thought of "myself", "my great achievements". We have to give up thoughts of being worshipped by disciples, of working miracles, etc. The attainment of real enlightenment means death; the death of me; my ego. After a series of disappointments perhaps we learn to give up ambition. We fall down and down until we reach the earth. We become like a grain of sand, simple, expecting nothing.

Our approach to everything becomes simple, and the teachings that we hear become workable. They encourage us to work as a grain of sand: without expectations or dreams.

> We have heard so many promises, have listened to so many alluring descriptions of exotic places of all kinds, have seen so many dreams, but from the point of view of a grain of sand, we could not care less. We are just a speck of dust in the midst of the universe. At the same time our situation is very spacious, very beautiful and workable. In fact, it is very inviting, inspiring. If you are a grain of sand, the rest of the universe, all the space, all the room is yours, because you obstruct nothing, overcrowd nothing, possess nothing. There is tremendous openness. You are the emperor of the universe because you are a grain of sand. The world is very simple and at the same time very dignified and open, because your inspiration is based upon disappointment, which is without the ambition of the ego.[5]

Sooner or later in religion a stripping is required and a darkness must be faced. This stripping takes many forms.

In youth or adolescence the sacrifice often means giving without strings to a cause, to a person or to an ideal. Later on it develops into that special type of giving, which is giving up. Giving up the illusions about the same cause, person or ideal we had given so much to before. As we approach death, of course, we have to give up something more than illusions. The stripping, the sacrifice, changes its form, but it is always there. It seems unpleasant, but without it religion becomes both very easy and very cheap.[6]

A man may be born, but in order to be born he must first die, and in order to die he must first awake.

When a man awakes he can die; when he dies he can be born.[7]

All these great "efforts" of mine had been a form of ego. What I needed to do was to "let go and let God", to make myself less so that He could live in me more. Simone Weil compares making spiritual efforts with the story of the tailor:

There are people whose manner of seeking God is like a man making leaps into the air in the hope that, if he jumps a little higher each time, he will end by staying up there and rising into heaven. This is a vain hope. In Grimm's tale of "The Valiant Little Tailor" there is a trial of strength between the little tailor and a giant. The giant hurls a stone high into the air, so that it takes a very, very long time to fall down again. The little tailor, who has a bird in his pocket, says he can do much better and that the stones he throws don't come down; and he releases his bird. Everything without wings always comes down to earth again. People who make athletic leaps towards heaven are too absorbed in the muscular effort to be able to look up to heaven; and in this matter the looking up is the one thing that counts. It is what makes God come down. And when God has come down to us He raises us, He gives us wings.[8]

There once lived in Tibet a very kind and generous man. One day a famous lama came to his village. The man got an audience with the lama, and knelt at his feet saying, "I would like to become an enlightened being so that I may help all being and devote myself to Buddha's teachings. What should I do?"

The lama, seeing that the man was sincere, told him to go to the mountains and spend his life praying and meditating. He also gave him a special prayer to chant, telling him if he recited this with great devotion, he would surely become an enlightened being. The man did as the lama instructed. He found a cave in the mountains and there he prayed and meditated for twenty years but still he had not become enlightened.

Then the lama came again to the village. The man went to see him again, and told him of his plight.

"I have prayed and meditated for twenty years in the mountain," he said, "and still I am no nearer enlightenment."

The lama looked solemn. "What were my instructions?" he asked. The man told him. "Oh," said the lama, "I am afraid that I must have told you the wrong thing. I am afraid that you will never be enlightened now."

The man fell at the lama's feet and wept. "I'm sorry", said the lama. "There's nothing I can do for you."

The man went back to his cave, feeling that twenty years of his life had been wasted.

"What shall I do?", he thought, "now that I must abandon hope of ever being enlightened?"

Then he sat in his meditation position, shut his eyes and thought, "I may as well carry on with my prayers and meditation – what else is there for me to do?"

So without any hope of enlightenment he began to pray.

Immediately, he became enlightened.

He saw the world in all its reality, everything was clear. He understood, at last, that it was only his grasping at enlightenment that prevented him from attaining it. Now he would be able to help all living beings find peace through his wisdom and compassion. Now he would leave his cave and go back into the world to spread the teachings of the Buddha.

He walked out of his cave and gazed at the village below. He had seen it so often before, but never so clearly as now. For a moment he thought he heard the soft laugh of the famous lama, as he looked up at the sky and the huge rainbow which was stretching its arc across the snowy peaks.[9]

This life, you must know as the tiny
  Splash of a raindrop,
A thing of beauty that disappears even
  As it comes into being.

Therefore, set your goal.
Make use of every day and night
  To achieve it.

Tsong Kapa

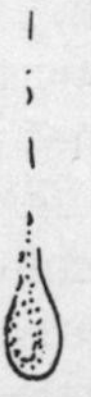

14

Prayer and Meditation

In everyone there is a yearning towards the light. The psychologist Carl Rogers was struck by the sight of potatoes in the cellar sending pale spindly shoots up towards the one small window, in a desperate groping for the light; this image helped him when he was dealing with his patients. He saw that even in the worst cases there was something in that person which was groping towards the light of being. But our reaching after spiritual things is feeble and intermittent in most of us. Often a prayer is simply begging God not to let 2+2=4. The fact that we are under the law of gravity, and many other laws, simply has to be accepted. However, instead of begging God to change our outside circumstances we could ask Him to change our inner circumstances, that is, to give us the inner support and strength we need in times of trouble. I have never known a prayer like that to go unanswered.

> One must learn to pray, just as one must learn everything else. Whoever knows how to pray and is able to concentrate in the proper way, his prayer can give results. But it must be understood that there are different prayers and that their results are different. This is known even from ordinary divine service. But when we speak of prayer or of the results of prayer we always imply only one kind of prayer – petition, or we think that petition can be united with all other kinds of prayers. This of course is not true. Most prayers have nothing in common with petitions. I speak of ancient prayers; many of them are much older than Christianity. These prayers are, so to speak, *recapitulations*; by

> repeating them aloud or to himself a man endeavours to experience what is in them, their whole content, with his mind and his feeling. And a man can always make new prayers for himself. For example a man says – "I want to be serious". But the whole point is in how he says it. If he repeats it even ten thousand times a day and is thinking of how soon he will finish and what will there be for dinner and the like, then it is not prayer but simply self-deceit.[1]

So often our prayers are concerned with what I want from God and not what God wants from me. I have noticed in my own case that sometimes my prayers are feeble, out of a kind of nervousness – I'm not really sure I want the Almighty to be listening: "It is a terrible thing to fall into the hands of the living God!"

At other times, when it seems I have tried to pray intensely, and yet I don't hear an answer, I remember a description I read of how we are like water-logged radios. We send out feeble bleeps from time to time, but in order to hear the answer clearly we need to clean the radio and set it in good working order. I discovered that meditation was a wonderful way of cleaning my receiving apparatus. Gradually my whirling thoughts began to grow less, and I became quieter, more able to hear the still, small voice. But I wanted to progress further by getting away from my busy social life. I made up my mind to go to the desert to meditate.

When I was installed there I sat by myself on a lonely mountain top, and I wondered what my friends were doing, and what they thought of me going, and whether everyone knew what I had done. Then I began to laugh – the busy social life that I had taken such pains to leave behind was still going on inside my head!

There is a Zen story about a man who begged the abbot to let him come to the monastery to meditate, because there were too many interruptions in his home. The abbot agreed, warning him however that there would still be interruptions in the monastery. The man came and sat in the great hall, which was almost too silent. He opened his eyes after a while to see what a tiny sound was. He saw the stick of incense burning and wondered why smoke always rises. He saw that the incense was a more expensive brand than at his local temple. He worked out what the monastery had paid for it, thinking that if they got a reduction for buying in quantity he might buy some from them at a lower price and sell to his local temple and make a small profit . . .

Then the bell rang. The meditation was over. He went to the abbot saying, "I understand. The interruptions are from within. From now on I shall practise meditation in my home. Please give me your blessing." The abbot blessed him, and he returned.[2]

Cecil Lewis, in his book *A Way to Be*, analyses the difficulties of meditation. In the dictionary the word meditation is defined as "to think deeply". But whenever we do try to think deeply, in a few seconds we find that our mind starts going off at a tangent thinking about something else, trivial or irrelevant. We bring our mind back and back to the problem, but within a short time, the mind is off again!

The reason for this is that in our usual state we do not really think at all. We have a very clever card index in our heads which relies on associations instead. The trouble is that the card index can take over our lives. We find ourselves going round and round in a circle, trapped by this mechanism in our heads. *I* do not think, rather "it thinks" in me! It goes on endlessly. There is only one way to stop it: to try to be quiet inside. Then we see even more clearly the "rush hour" going on in our heads. This can bring about a real longing to be still.

To see that we need to be quiet is a very big step, it can give rise to a sincere determination to find a moment of quiet in every day; that is to practise meditation. But how?

> Every aim has a technique . . . the first and most important part of this technique . . . lies in posture. The outside reflects the inside. Our way of standing, walking, sitting,

> shows how we are. A man with a hurried walk, is hurrying inside – a man flopped in an easy chair is slouching inside. Quietness is not to flop, to give up. So first, I sit up. My spine is erect. I carry my head well. I am intensely alert – but I do not move. . . . In a moment I shall be lost again in my dreams. But then I have an idea. It is a trick, really . . . If I could give my head something to do, that might tether it, control it, make it my servant not my master. I mustn't leave a vacuum. Nature abhors it. I must occupy my mind, give it something, not perhaps what it wants to do, but what it can do. The odds are against me, of course. The weak, struggling part that wants something different has been, all our lives, at the mercy of this demon in our heads.
>
> But I have my bait, my trick: I give it something to do. I invite it, for instance, to count . . . I suggest it watch my breathing – without altering it – I give it a short prayer to repeat "Lord have mercy upon me", or I take it on a tour of my body, inviting it to watch over the relaxing of my limbs, one by one, in turn. It works. With such things I can tether my mind.[3]

This work can change our lives, but only if it is done in secret. We must neither impose ourselves on those for whom such work would have no meaning, nor try to impress others with our achievements. This idea of meditating has been known for a long time, even in the West. The Roman Emperor Marcus Aurelius wrote hundreds of years ago:

> Men seek out retreats for themselves, cottages in the country, lonely seashores and mountains. Thou too art disposed to hanker after such things: and yet all this is the very commonest stupidity; for it is in thy power, whenever thou wilt, to retire into thyself: and nowhere is there any place whereto a man may retire quieter and more free from politics than his own soul; above all if he have within him thoughts such as he only need regard attentively to be at perfect ease: and that ease is nothing else than a well

> ordered mind. Constantly then use this retreat, and renew thyself therein: and be thy principles brief and elementary, which, as soon as ever thou recur to them, will suffice to wash thy soul entirely clean, and send thee back without vexation to whatsoever awaiteth thee.[4]

Unless we cultivate the life of the spirit, it will not grow. We have taken it for granted that men have souls – but what does that mean? Is it not just that men have a possibility to have a soul? But can we say that a possibility is the same as a fact? Margaret Anderson had an insight into this:

> I saw that you can't say a man is born with a soul any more than you can say that he is born with an art. A man may be born an artist – that is, with an art tendency – but he won't have an art until he has worked at art, developed it through an organic process of growth. He must live a life of Art. In the same way, a man can't have a soul until he has lived a life of the Soul.[5]

> Now is liberation, illumination, or that enlightenment reserved only for the extraordinary few? Or if you had that tremendous insight into the wholeness of life would your consciousness be totally different? Naturally it would, because that liberating insight frees you from all the content of that consciousness – the pain, the anxiety, the loneliness, sorrow, depression, all that is wiped out. It is a fact if you do it, and it can be done. And it is not reserved for the few. But we human beings are not persistent, we do not apply ourselves continuously, we are slack. We do this one day and we are weary of it the next, we slack off. So the ball is never in our court, it is always in other people's courts.[6]

I saw the importance of "growing a soul" and I wanted to learn to be quiet inside, but what I came up against was my great need and wish for excitement. Once I got used to meditation and it wasn't new and exciting, I became restless. I saw at last that I wanted to run away, that all my life I had been running away – in case I had to encounter myself. My fear of boredom was a fear of meeting myself – and finding a vacuum!

> Boredom has many aspects: there is the sense that nothing is happening, that something might happen, or even that what we would like to happen might replace that which is not happening. Or, one might appreciate boredom as a delight. The practice of meditation could be described as relating with cool boredom, refreshing boredom, boredom like a mountain stream. It refreshes because we do not have to do anything or expect anything. But there must be some sense of discipline if we are to get beyond the frivolity of trying to replace boredom.
>
> That is why we work with the breath as our practice of meditation. Simply relating with the breath is very monotonous and unadventurous – we do not discover that the third eye is opening or that *cakras* are unfolding. It is like a stone-carved Buddha sitting in the desert. Nothing, absolutely nothing, happens.
>
> As we realize that nothing is happening, strangely we begin to realize that something dignified is happening. There is no room for frivolity, no room for speed. We just breathe and are there. There is something very satisfying and wholesome about it.[7]

The fear of boredom had pursued me all my life, driven me to parties, excitement, T.V., over-eating and drinking . . . but I was getting tired of running away. I wanted something more in my life even if this meant accepting the boredom, and working through it.

> We've never really accepted boredom as a conscious state. As soon as it comes into the mind we start looking for something interesting, something pleasant. But in meditation we're allowing boredom to be. We're allowing ourselves to be fully consciously bored, fully depressed, fed up, jealous, angry, disgusted. All the nasty unpleasant

> experiences of life that we have repressed out of consciousness and never really looked at, never really accepted, we begin to accept into consciousness – not as personality problems any more but just out of compassion. Out of kindness and wisdom we allow things to take their natural course to cessation, rather than just keep them going round in the same old cycles of habit.[8]

When I gave up all expectation of being excited and interested, and accepted the possibility that I would be bored, things changed for me. I discovered a new world. It was very simple and fresh, like a child's world, and ordinary things seemed very attractive. This also happened to Ajahn Sumedho, a Buddhist abbot. He had been depressed and had gone away to meditate by himself.

> The next morning when I woke from sleep and looked around, I felt that everything I saw was beautiful. Everything, even the most unbeautiful detail, was beautiful. I was in a state of awe. The hut itself was a crude structure, not beautiful by anyone's standards, but it looked to me like a palace. The scrubby looking trees outside looked like a most beautiful forest. Sunbeams were streaming through the window on to a plastic dish and the plastic dish looked beautiful! That sense of beauty stayed with me for about a week and then reflecting on it I suddenly realized that that's the way things really are when the mind is clear.
>
> When we get used to looking through a dirty window everything seems grey, grimy and ugly. Meditation is a way of cleaning the window, purifying the mind, allowing things to come up into consciousness and letting them go. Then with the wisdom faculty, the Buddha wisdom, we observe how things really are. It's not just attaching to beauty, to purity of mind, but actually understanding. It is wisely reflecting on the way nature operates so that we are no longer deluded by it into creating habits for our life through ignorance.[9]

Suzuki, a Zen Buddhist who left Japan to found a Buddhist centre in San Francisco, called it being "Nothing special".

> At Eiheiji monastery, when we had to sit, we sat; when we had to bow to Buddha, we bowed to Buddha. That is all. And when we were practising, we did not feel anything special. We did not even feel that we were leading a monastic life. For us, the monastic life was the usual life, and the people who came from the city were unusual people. When we saw them we felt, "Oh, some unusual people have come!"
>
> But once I had left Eiheiji and been away for some time, coming back was different. I heard the various sounds of practice – the bells and the monks reciting the sutra – and I had a deep feeling. There were tears flowing out of my eyes, nose, and mouth! It is the people who are outside of the monastery who feel its atmosphere. I think this is true for everything. When we hear the sound of the pine trees on a windy day, perhaps the wind is just blowing, and the pine tree is just standing in the wind. That is all that they are doing. But the people who listen to the wind in the tree will write a poem, or will feel something unusual. That is, I think, the way everything is.[10]

The reason that we have to learn to be quiet and make a space in ourselves is so that God's Spirit can come and live there. There is nothing in us otherwise of any real worth. As Christ has told us, "Only God is good".

"God dwells wherever man lets him in."

This is the ultimate purpose: to let God in. But we can let Him in only where we really stand, where we live, where we live a true life. If we maintain holy intercourse with the little world entrusted to us, if we help the holy spiritual substance to accomplish itself in that section of Creation in which we are living, then we are establishing, in this our place, a dwelling for the Divine Presence.[11]

A master of meditation was instructing some devotees. He said that freedom from strong reactions, an attitude of reverence, and regular meditation would help them realize the divine life pervading all things.

He finished by saying that this realization of divine life must pervade all their daily life; the process was like filling a sieve with water. After he left the group discussed what he could have meant. One said angrily, "He's telling us we'll never do it. Filling a sieve with water is exactly what happens to me now. I go to hear a sermon, or I pray, I feel uplifted for a moment, and my character improves for a bit, but then I forget and I am back to where I started. It is like filling a sieve with water."

They argued among themselves but they could not agree what was meant by this saying. Some thought he was laughing at them, some thought he was telling them that there was something fundamentally wrong with their ideas. Others thought he might be referring to something in the classics. They looked for reference to a sieve, but couldn't find any. In the end they forgot about the whole thing, except for one woman who made up her mind to see the master.

When she questioned him, he gave her a sieve and a cup, and went with her to the seashore nearby, where they stood on a rock together.

"Show me how you would fill the sieve with water", he said.

She bent down and tried to scoop up the water with the sieve into the cup. No sooner did the water come into the sieve than it was gone again.

"It's just like that with spiritual practice too," he said, "while one stands on the rock of I-ness, and tries to ladle the divine realization into it. That's not the way to fill the sieve with water, or the self with divine life."

"How do you, do it then?" she asked.

He took the sieve from her hand, and threw it far out into the sea, where it floated momentarily and then sank.

"Now it's full of water," he said, "and it will remain so. That's the way to fill it with water, and it's the way to do spiritual practice. It's not ladling little cupfuls of divine life into the individuality, but throwing the individuality far out into the sea of divine life."[12]

15

Paying Attention

A lot of the value I got from reading spiritual philosophy derived from the East was that it put everything in the new way, and so it was easier to pay attention to what was being said. To perceive an old truth in a new way is just as good as perceiving a new truth. Chesterton was once told that soon communicating with the distant stars would seem as ordinary to us as talking on the telephone. "If only", he exclaimed, "talking on the telephone could seem to us as miraculous as communing with the distant stars!"

Then I became aware that this attention, this perceiving of things freshly at the moment, was the key to everything of importance.

> Not only does the love of God have attention for its substance; the love of our neighbour, which we know to be the same love, is made of this same substance. Those who are unhappy have no need for anything in this world but people capable of giving them their attention. The capacity to give one's attention to a sufferer is a very rare and difficult thing; it is almost a miracle; it *is* a miracle. Nearly all those who think they have this capacity do not possess it. Warmth of heart, impulsiveness, pity are not enough.
>
> In the first legend of the Grail, it is said that the Grail (the miraculous stone vessel which satisfies all hunger by virtue of the consecrated host) belongs to the first comer who asks the guardian of the vessel, a king three-quarters paralysed by the most painful wound: "What are you going through?"

> The love of our neighbour in all its fullness simply means being able to say to him: "What are you going through?" . . . it is enough, but it is indispensable, to know how to look at him in a certain way.
>
> This way of looking is first of all attentive. The soul empties itself of all its own contents in order to receive into itself the being it is looking at, just as he is in all his truth.
>
> Only he who is capable of attention can do this.[1]

Attention can be developed in many ways. It is a way of directing our minds more consciously. In that way, even consciously directed intellectual efforts can help.

> Never in any case whatever is a genuine effort of the attention wasted. It always has its effect on the spiritual plane and in consequence on the lower one of the intelligence, for all spiritual light lightens the mind.
>
> If we concentrate our attention on trying to solve a problem of geometry, and if at the end of an hour we are no nearer to doing so than at the beginning, we have nevertheless been making progress each minute of that hour in another more mysterious dimension. Without our knowing or feeling it, this apparently barren effort has brought more light into the soul. The result will one day be discovered in prayer.[2]

The American Indian has been aware of the importance of directed attention for many years. In *The Sacred Pipe* Black Elk tells of a sacred ritual in which the young initiate receives the message "Be attentive", and the holy man leading the ceremony continues:

> Grandfather, this young man who has offered the pipe to You, has heard a voice which said to him, "be attentive as you walk!" He wants to know what this message means; it must now be explained to him. It means that he should always remember You, *O Wakan-Tanka,* as he walks the

> sacred path of life; and he must be attentive to all the signs that You have given to us. If he does this always, he will become wise and a leader of his people. *O Wakan-Tanka*, help us all to be always attentive!*

> This message – "Be attentive!" – well expresses a spirit which is central to the Indian peoples; it implies that in every act, in every thing, and in every instant, the Great Spirit is present, and that one should be continually and intensely "attentive" to this Divine presence.
>
> This presence of *Waken-Tanka*, and one's consciousness of it, is that which the Christian saints have termed "living in the moment", the "eternal now".[3]

The message "Be Attentive" could equally be said to be the aim of Zen practice.

> Zen, seeks not to *explain* but to *pay attention*, to *become aware*, to be *mindful*, in other words to develop a certain *kind of consciousness that is above and beyond deception* by verbal formulas – or by emotional excitement.[4]

Emotional excitement makes attention impossible. It is necessary to quieten something in ourselves;

> Quietness is not a passive state. It is not just lolling in a chair and doing nothing. It has to be fought for. As soon as I try it, I am assailed by the whole momentum of my ordinary life, which is not used to quiet, which hates silence . . .
>
> My machine, my normal functions, are designed to

associate. That is their job. If I am to quiet them, I must give them something to do. Not perhaps what they want to do; but what they can be persuaded to put up with. It is a trick to stop them frittering away all my energies.

All religions propose different techniques to meet this difficulty. One that I have followed for thirty years is to place my attention in each of my limbs in turn . . . trying intently to relax my muscles which – I soon find – are tense and difficult to let go. All my life, for this time, is within my limbs, persistently insisting, relaxing them little by little. And so I begin to be quiet.

Of course I fail! My mind takes off in all directions. But I have my weapon: my *attention*. I come back.

So we arrive at a strange, simple realization. The first step towards the Kingdom of Heaven lies in my power to control my attention. Unless I learn to control my attention, nothing is possible for me.[5]

It seems that everything hangs on attention, it seems such an ordinary word; making me think of all the times in school that I was ordered to "pay attention!"

Yet perhaps there is something in that – attention seems to be a coin that you can pay with – to buy the pearl of great price!

I want to be attentive – to be here at the moment – but I keep forgetting. In the struggle to remember, my body can help me. I can bring my attention to my feet, for example, and sense my soles on the floor. I am brought back to the moment – NOW! Then this sensation fades or I forget again; but now I can sense my fingertips; again I can be present NOW. I try to come back to the sensation of myself as often as I can; it is my prayer;

> Conscience calls me to be myself.
> To be myself begins with self-knowledge.
> Self-knowledge begins with work on myself.
> Work on myself is based on the sensation of myself.[6]

We can practise attention to strengthen it, but it is important to start on small things.

> Your nervous and restless movements make everyone know, consciously or unconsciously, that you have no authority and are a booby. With these restless movements you cannot be anything. The first thing for you to do is to stop these movements. Make this your aim, your God. Even get your family to help you. Only after this, you can perhaps gain attention. This is an example of doing . . .
>
> Try to accomplish very small things. If at first you aim at big things you will never be anything.[7]

I saw that to pay attention I needed the help of my body – but I had always despised it! I wanted to be a pure spirit and it seemed to me that my body was holding me down, with its greed, its laziness and wayward desires.

One night I had a dream. In the dream I wanted to soar upward and fly, but I couldn't because my heavy legs were holding me down to the ground. Someone handed me a knife and suggested that I cut off my legs; then I would be able to fly I agreed, and cut them off. When they were severed from me, dripping with blood, I saw in horror what I had done. Far from being able to fly, I was crippled for life. I would never walk again! When I woke up I could hardly believe that my legs were still there. I had been given another chance! I was so glad to see my legs attached to me again – large and pink and unharmed!

From then on I changed my attitude to my body. I stopped taking it for granted and began to appreciate it more. I saw that the dream had been telling me to stop trying to soar to Heaven. It seemed that I would have to try to get there along with my body; "Brother Ass" as St Francis calls it. I had to accept the humiliation of seeing how often I was at the mercy of the body's wants and needs – and this was a salutary lesson. The body keeps us humble.

I came to realize that my body, far from holding me back, was the most important link with reality that I had. In my head I might dream that I possessed great spiritual strength, but my body quickly showed me where I really stood.

Another thing I noticed was how often I changed; my moods, feelings, likes and dislikes all varied from day to day – only my body was the same every day. This provided me with a point of reference. In struggling with the demands of my body, I learned that the best way was not to oppose the body's wishes directly, for that only aroused opposition in myself. Far better was to ask God's help in prayer; then something was helped without any opposing struggle.

> We have never regarded our bodies as sacred property. The attitude of sacredness has been neglected, particularly in the Western world. Instead, life is regarded as a hassle. We were born, breast-fed or bottle-fed, and put into diapers. Those were our unpleasant facts of life. Now we can go to the toilet and drink our cup of tea – how victorious we are! We view it as a victory that we have survived all that. But we have not actually developed any art in our lives. We do not know how to care for our bodies.
>
> We may have been taught sophisticated table manners by our aristocratic parents. They may have taught us how to drink, how to use forks and knives, and how to sit properly and make good conversation . . . we have been taught a façade, rather than what should be felt. We could be extremely well-mannered and able to pass through diplomatic circles. Nevertheless there could still be a crudeness of fundamentally not knowing how to relate with our cup of tea, our plate our table or our chair . . .We learn to be perfect actors. It does not matter how we feel. We might be in tears, but still we put on a gleaming smile and make

> polite conversation. If we cannot find anything good to talk about, we just talk about the weather. With that approach, we become very crude. In fact, we are trying to become perfect actors rather than real people.[8]

It is important to be sincere, even in bodily functions; a zen master was defined in these terms: "When he eats, he eats. When he sleeps he sleeps."

> The most important point is to own your own physical body. If you slump, you will lose yourself. Your mind will be wandering about somewhere else; you will not be in your body. This is not the way. We must exist right here, right now! This is the key point. You must have your own body and mind. Everything should exist in the right place, in the right way. Then there is no problem. If the microphone I use when I speak exists somewhere else, it will not serve its purpose. When we have our body and mind in order, everything else will exist in the right place, in the right way.
>
> So try always to keep the right posture, not only when you practise zazen, but in all your activities. Take the right posture when you are driving your car, and when you are reading. If you read in a slumped position, you cannot stay awake long. Try. You will discover how important it is to keep the right posture.[9]

We have got into the habit of admiring people who can do ten things at once; never mind if all of them are done badly, and that is the very opposite of real attention.

> Always do only one thing at a time, that of the present moment. But do it well, be in it entirely . . . Too bad if meanwhile business worth many millions waits at the door . . . Man is always doing seven things at once; if he does as I say, even for one little thing, the other six will look after themselves.[10]

Attention can be practised in the most ordinary actions, in fact, the more ordinary, the better.

One day, after I looked for my cup of tea and found that I had drunk it without noticing, I made a resolve to try to taste each bite of the food that I was eating. It was extraordinarily difficult. At first I found that I was so busy thinking about the next bite that I wasn't tasting what was actually in my mouth; in the next moment I'd disappeared into my dreaming thoughts, and the food had vanished without me noticing – just as the tea had done!

> If work becomes part of your spiritual practice, then your regular, daily problems cease to be only problems and become a source of inspiration. Nothing is rejected as ordinary and nothing is taken as being particularly sacred, but all the substance and material available in life-situations is used.
>
> True work is acting practically, relating to the earth directly. You could be working in the garden, in the house, washing dishes or doing whatever demands your attention. If you do not feel the relationship between earth and yourself, then the situation is going to turn chaotic. If you do not feel that every step, every situation reflects your state of mind, and therefore has spiritual significance, then the pattern of your life becomes full of problems, and you begin to wonder where these problems come from. They seem to spring from nowhere because you refuse to see the subtlety of life. Somehow, you cannot cheat, you cannot pretend to pour a cup of tea beautifully, you cannot act it. You must actually feel it, feel the earth and your relationship to it.[11]

I found that work could be very interesting if I tried to do it with real attention; so often I would "wake up" while doing the housework to find that all the time I had been living in a daydream.

One morning I was feeling very depressed. I was faced with

a pile of shirts to iron, and I was about to switch on the radio, as I usually did to listen to a play, when I had the thought of trying to iron these shirts with real attention. I took up the iron and felt, as if for the first time, the crispness of the white linen as the wrinkles were smoothed out of it. My hands enjoyed guiding the iron over the material, and in this simple enjoyment, my depression lifted. I saw to my surprise that working with attention could turn a chore into a pleasure, and give me energy instead of taking it away.

A young Dutchman who had gone to Japan to be a Zen monk describes his struggles in his book, *The Empty Mirror*. At one point he is being scolded by the head monk, being told that he must try to practise "right awareness".

> The monastic training tries to wake us up, but when it is time to sleep you may sleep. But when you are asleep, be awake. When you are cleaning vegetables, you really have to clean them. The idea is to throw the good pieces into the pot and the rotten pieces into the tin, not the other way around. Whatever you do, do it well, as well as you can, and be aware of what you are doing. Don't try to do two things at the same time, like pissing and cleaning your teeth. I have seen you do that. Perhaps you think you are saving time that way, but the result is no more than a mess in the lavatory and a mess in your mouth.

The new monk agreed to try, whereupon the head monk said, "You mustn't try, you must just do it".

Then he added that if the new monk ever succeeded in becoming aware, he should be careful not to let it go to his head. He told a story about a temple priest who was teaching a young man and used daily events as examples. One day there was a strong earthquake and a part of the temple collapsed, but the priest remarked calmly to his pupil:

> "Look, now you have been able to see how a Zen man behaves under stress. You will have noticed that I didn't

panic. I was quite aware of what was happening. I took you by the arm and we went to the kitchen, because that is the strongest part of the temple. I was proved right because the kitchen is still in one piece and we have survived the earthquake – we aren't even wounded. That I, in spite of my self-control and awareness, did suffer a slight shock, you may have deduced from the fact that I drank a large glass of water, something I would never do under normal circumstances."

The young man didn't say anything but smiled.

"What's so funny?" the priest asked.

"That wasn't water, reverend Sir," the young man said, "that was a very large glass of soy sauce."[12]

16

Creativity

The moment of creation is very satisfying. As in Genesis, faced with a void, the artist, with a bit of coloured mud creates a whole universe – sky, sea, clouds, land, people, even emotions and thoughts. It seems miraculous even to the one who is doing it.

I could never explain where the urge to paint comes from inside me, but it has always been there. My mother relates a story about me as a baby crying in the night. She went to my cot, thinking something was wrong, but when she turned on the light I, being too young to talk, pointed at the crayons and paper out of my reach. She put them into my crib and left me happily colouring!

The wish to paint feels like a hunger, or a longing for something that is just out of reach, something that I once had perhaps or hope to have in the future. It is like trying to remember a beautiful tune, and when the painting is going well it is as if I am remembering the tune. The melody is always there, but I have to find my way back to it. Michelangelo said about his sculpture: "The statue is always there, hidden in the block of marble. I only work to reveal it." At one's best moments one feels that the painting was always there waiting to be revealed, and one only has to uncover it without getting in the way.

It took me years to see how I "got in my own way". Laziness to begin with. Together with the longing to paint is something in me that runs away from all the effort involved. Anything that demands a finer effort is suddenly too much. I would rather do housework or go shopping. Tomorrow would be a better time to start! It takes a long time before I can see that tomorrow's painting is not a substitute for the work that I can do today. Tomorrow I am a different person. Then I might well have indigestion or an influx of visitors. If I use today, when I am prompted to paint, I can make a start which will help me tomorrow when I may be too unwell to do more than routine background work. Tomorrow a different side of my personality may be uppermost; and therefore the painting I could have done today, if not done now, is lost forever.

Even when I bring my unruly self to the easel and begin work, I continue to get in my own way. My attention wanders. I need all my attention for the painting but instead I am making up my shopping list, or wondering why my friend hasn't phoned.

I try to drop everything that is in the way.

When I am sitting at the easel and looking at what I am to paint, I see in a different way. I became aware of this through an experience I had at an Aikido class. The teacher told us to sit down for a moment and look at our surroundings. He asked us if we could see anything that was not necessary. I was taken aback by the question. I looked around the room again, and realized that when I had first come in I had grabbed with my eyes at a picture of a Japanese flowering cherry tree on a calendar, and rejected the stained hardboard walls. But now when I looked again I saw that the hardboard was necessary. It kept us secure, and even the stains represented the laws of heat and cold, wet and dry, in action.

The only time I really look at things is when I begin to paint. Then the staleness falls from my eyes, and I am able to look at everything as if seeing it for the first time. This shows me that for most of my life I live in a dream, grabbing with my eyes at what attracts me and discarding what does not.

The moment of creation gives me a kind of grace. I am lifted out of my petty self and at that moment am able to look at what is in front of me with impartial attention. This attention, this accepting of everything for what it is, is a kind of love. At this moment as a painter I can love the water for its wetness, the glass for its hardness, the wood for its weathered lines and cracks. No face is ugly in itself, just as no tree is ugly. We speak of attention as something that we "give" and "receive". We speak of it as a gift, which it is. To give attention is to create a space within which the other can reveal itself to me.

> The painter's instructions might be: spend ten years observing bamboos, become a bamboo yourself, then forget everything and – paint.[1]

When the painting comes from the right place in myself I am often surprised by the result. This surprise is a kind of shock of recognition, which is connected with the first longing that made me want to paint. The longing is for order – not tidiness, but a pattern or rhythm that seems to echo a greater pattern in the universe.

When I was going through a difficult time, an analogy came to me: to suffer without meaning is like being carved up by thugs, to suffer with meaning is like undergoing a necessary operation by a surgeon; even if he has no anaesthetic, the operation is bearable because it has meaning.

This is why all real art is so deeply satisfying. It hints at a meaning in the universe, and gives us hope that we are undergoing something that can be for our ultimate good, that we are not just at the mercy of random thugs.

Carpet-makers in the Orient always leave a break in the pattern somewhere, a space for the soul to escape. Equally, there should be an element of something left out or mysterious in the painting, to show us that the longing can never be satisfied completely.

Sometimes one of my pupils asks whether he should try to develop a "style" of painting. I always tell the pupil that if one just paints as well as one can, the style will happen by itself. To try self-consciously to adopt a particular style is to move away from the inner artist in oneself. Style is something that everyone else should be able to see, but not the artist concerned. He or she should be simply painting from the self.

Because God is always original, each person is unique, and the nearer each person gets to painting from the real self, the more original the work becomes.

> When a man embarks on something great, in the spirit of truth, he need not be afraid that another may imitate him. But if he does not do so in the spirit of truth, but plans to act in a way that no one else can imitate, then he drags the great down to the lowest level – and everyone can do the same.[2]

Being oneself is not at all the same thing as the self-congratulation of vanity. Vanity is to do with the superficial posturing of the ego, but if one can be true to the deepest level of self, one approaches the nearness of the indwelling of the Holy Spirit, and as He dwells in all of us, what point is there in vanity?

> Self-satisfaction, self-contentment, lack of determined effort and above all lack of ecstasy in any pursuit, is the essence of mediocrity.[3]

One of the curious things I have noticed in my many years of teaching painting, is that it is not necessarily the ones with the most natural talent who become the best artists. What matters most is determination or stick-at-ivity, people who keep working, but with a certain intelligence – that is, they try not to repeat mistakes – and with humility – that is, they will accept criticism. It is those people who will eventually find their authentic voice.

I asked some artist friends of mine what art meant to them. One said, "Art is nothing if it is not an expression of love – both in those who do it and those who appreciate it." Another friend answered, "No, love by itself does not include the hate; real art must reflect the whole thing, good and bad. It must include passion and pain. Every person has all that in him, and great art would be a revealing of the whole inner world of the artist. It is a communication without words. It is not necessary to like the work of the artist, but something must be communicated that is real."

The work of art then acquires a life of its own, and can go on exerting an influence after the artist is dead. The creative process is still creating its effect on those who see it through the work of art.

The nearer the artist gets to revealing his own inner truth, the more it reflects the truth of the outer world. Sometimes the artist can be the medium through which the future prophesies itself: as when the breaking down of the formal rules in painting foretold the breaking up of the old order in society. In all real art there is a large element of prophecy; there is a mystery there that lures and attracts us, but we cannot completely comprehend it.

There is a sense in which all the arts have a possibility of reflecting the spiritual.

> The gradual progress of all creation from a lower to a higher evolution, its change from one aspect to another, is shown as in music where a melody is transposed from one key into another. The friendship and enmity among men, and their likes and dislikes, are as chords and discords. The harmony of human nature, and the human tendency to attraction and repulsion, are like the effect of the constant and dissonant intervals in music . . .
>
> The Emperor asked the musician one day, "Tell me what raga, what mode did your master sing?" Tansen told him the name of the raga, and sang it for him, but the emperor was not content, saying, "Yes, it is the same music, but it is not the same spirit. Why is this?" The musician replied, "The reason is this, that while I sing before you, the

> Emperor of this country, my Master sings before God; that is the difference."[4]

Today most artists are preoccupied with "expressing themselves". Our civilization has forgotten the high aims of the artists in the past, as when noble cathedrals were built, some taking a hundred years, so that the architect knew that he would never see his work completed.

> . . . all artists . . . should be anonymous, detached from all that they create. I think that is the greatest truth. To be, to give and to be detached from what you give. You see what I mean? After all, the greatest artists of the world, the greatest teachers of the world say: "Look here, I have got something which, if you really understand it, would forever unfold your intelligence, would act as your intuition. But don't worship me as an individual – I am not concerned, after all." But most artists want their names put under the picture, they want to be admired. They want their degrees and titles.[5]

This appears to me to be the greatest humility, when an artist can work for God so selflessly, that he or she does not even want to put a name on it. Needless to say, I haven't got there yet! But as I get older I can begin to "see through" the trappings of success a little more clearly.

> There are perhaps three kinds of creation. The first is to be aware of ourselves after we finish zazen. When we sit we are nothing, we do not even realize what we are; we just sit. But when we stand up, we are there! That is the first

step in creation. When you are there, everything else is there; everything is created all at once. When we emerge from nothing, when everything emerges from nothing, we see it all as a fresh new creation. This is non-attachment. The second kind of creation is when you act, or produce or prepare something like food or tea. The third kind is to create something within yourself, such as education, or culture, or art, or some system for your society. So there are three kinds of creation. But if you forget the first, the most important one, the other two will be like children who have lost their parents; their creation will mean nothing.[6]

17

Children

Having my three children was the most powerful experience in my life, but it was a strangely impersonal one. I felt from the beginning of pregnancy that I didn't own my body any more, strange things happened to it over which I had no control; and when the time came for the delivery, my body knew what to do and I did not.

This feeling of impersonality continued as I became known by the anonymous title of "Mother". I had ceased to be my particular self, Brigid. There were moments when I resented this, when I struggled to be "myself" in the midst of the morass of raising three boys very close in age to each other. But then I saw that this impersonal feeling was showing me something. In having my children I was serving something bigger than myself: "Nature" or "mankind". As the children got older I began to see with greater clarity that they were not mine at all.

And a woman who held a babe against her bosom said,
Speak to us of Children.
And he said:
Your children are not your children.
They are the sons and daughters of Life's longing for itself.

> They come through you but not from you,
> And though they are with you yet they belong not to you.
>
> You may give them your love but not your thoughts,
> For they have their own thoughts.
> You may house their bodies but not their souls,
> For their souls dwell in the house of tomorrow, which you cannot visit, not even in your dreams.
> You may strive to be like them, but seek not to make them like you.
> For life goes not backward nor tarries with yesterday.
> You are the bows form which your children as living arrows are sent forth.[1]

The children did not belong to me, nor did they belong to themselves. I felt a great mystery in each newborn child, as if he were still very close to God. In many Eastern religions they believe that we know everything before we are born, and that birth is a kind of forgetting.

> Before a child is born, a light is held behind its head with which it can see from one end of the world to the other, and they teach it the whole of the Torah. But at the moment of birth an angel touches it on the lips, and it forgets all. So all of life is spent remembering what we once knew.[2]

The children were persons, imprisoned and inarticulate in their small bodies, and it was my job, as much as I could, to help them to emerge. Sometimes I failed them when they needed me. Sometimes I was preoccupied or neglectful, but they were very forgiving. Above all, I tried to give them the feeling that they were truly loved for themselves. This is the only real necessity.

> The child lying with half-closed eyes, waiting with tense soul for its mother to speak to it – the mystery of its will is not directed towards enjoying (or dominating) a person, or towards doing something of its own accord; but towards experiencing communion in face of the lonely night, which spreads beyond the window and threatens to invade. But many children do not need to wait, for they know that they are unceasingly addressed in a dialogue which never breaks off. In face of the lonely night which threatens to invade, they lie preserved and guarded, invulnerable, clad in the silver mail of trust.
>
> Trust, trust in the world, because this human being exists – that is the most inward achievement of the relation in education. Because this human being exists, meaninglessness, however hard pressed you are by it, cannot be the real truth. Because this human being exists, in the darkness the light lies hidden, in fear salvation, and in the callousness of one's fellow men the great Love.[3]

> When a father complained to the Baalshem: "My son has departed from God, what shall I do?" he answered: "Love him the more."[4]

A child who knows that he is loved can also believe in the love of God. There is a story about a Zen nun who was beloved for her gifts of sympathy and far-sightedness. She was asked how she came to dedicate her life to the Religious life. She said that, although orphaned at a very young age, she had been brought up by her aunt who was a nun in charge of a temple. Although devoted to the little girl, the aunt could not give her as much time as she wanted to, because of her own religious duties. So she took the little girl to the great statue of Buddha in the temple, who was seated with his fingers forming a circle. She asked the Buddha to watch over the child, and when they had left the temple together the aunt told the child, "If you ever do anything wrong, which would make the Buddha angry, go and try to do something good to show that you are sorry; such as tidying up. Then run and look at the Buddha. If he is angry, his fingers will make sharp angles, but if he has forgiven you, they will be a circle as they are now."

The nun said that this had made a big impression on her as a child. Many times she rushed to the temple and hastily swept the garden, then she crept in to the temple and took a frightened peep at the Buddha's fingers. It was always such a relief when she saw the circle and knew that she was forgiven.

> At this point one of her listeners demurred, arguing:
>
> "I don't approve of using this sort of superstitious falsehood to control the actions of children. They only react against it all when they find out they have been deceived. Didn't you, yourself, have a reaction of anger and scepticism when you found out that the fingers of the Buddha never move at all?"
>
> The nun replied: "Oh, it wasn't a falsehood. My aunt would never have told a falsehood. When I found that the Buddha never does move his fingers, I realized that the Buddha always forgives. Even at the moment of weakness or sin, the Buddha forgives. He is never angry. And it made me feel that I didn't want to cause the Buddha to forgive and forgive; I wanted to live so that he would not have to forgive. It was a great help in some crisis of temptation and fear. That's what my aunt wanted me to understand by the fingers."[5]

Sometimes I worried about the fact that because we had a sick child in the family, I could not shelter the other children from a great deal of trauma and suffering. But I found that they learned to cope with this, and in the learning they grew into more understanding.

> It even seems as if young people who have had a hard struggle for existence are spared inner problems, while those who for some reason or other have no difficulty with adaptation run into problems of sex or conflicts arising from a sense of inferiority.[6]

In the Tibetan tradition if a child is discovered to be an Incarnation then he is taken away from his family at a very young age, and trained to be a monk and a Rinpoche. Chogyam Trungpa was such an Incarnation, and he describes his life as a little boy. From the age of eighteen months, when he was taken away from his family, he had a tutor who never left him, even sleeping outside his door at night so that the little boy could not get out. He was constantly criticized, told to sit up if he leaned back, told to welcome visiting dignitaries and converse with them.

> I was constantly cut down. I had been brought up strictly since infancy, from the age of eighteen months, so that I had no other reference point such as the idea of freedom or being loose. I had no idea what it was like to be an ordinary child playing in the dirt or playing with toys or chewing on rusted metal or whatever . . . The only time I was not being watched was when I went to the bathroom. It was my one free time. Usually I would feel an enormous rush of fresh air, because bathrooms were built overhanging cliffs and had big holes in the floor. I would feel the fresh air coming up, and at the same time I would know that nobody was watching me, telling me how to defecate properly. Apart from that, I was always watched. Even when I ate, I was watched and told how to eat properly, how to extend my arm, how to watch the cup, how to bring it to my mouth. If I made a big noise while swallowing, I was criticized for eating "crocodile style". I was told that Rinpoches, or other important tulkus, were not supposed to swallow crocodile style.[7]

But he goes on to say that suddenly he stopped struggling against authority, and began to develop. He asked more and more questions from his tutors, and eventually they ran out of answers. They became bothered by him because he was so intense. They could not keep up with him anymore. He had found that he had become a part of the teachings himself, an embodiment of them; and he was no longer disturbed by his teachers.

To our ideas, his description of his childhood sounds as if he had been treated harshly, but a child can put up with a great deal of hardship, if he senses the basic goodness of those who are dealing with him. What seems to damage a child is the hidden evil in people:

> Children have an almost uncanny instinct for the teacher's personal shortcomings. They know the false from the true far better than one likes to admit. Therefore the teacher should watch his own psychic condition, so that he can spot the source of the trouble when anything goes wrong with the children entrusted in his care. He himself may easily be the unconscious cause of evil.[8]

When I was ten years old, our family moved to Montreal. A young and beautiful nun, Sister Rose, was the teacher in my new school. The school had a very mixed group of children, and among my new friends was a daughter of poor Italian immigrants. She was called Maria. Sister Rose and Maria did not like each other. Maria was the only girl who didn't have a crush on Sister Rose.

Often I was the fortunate girl to be singled out by Sister Rose because I drew pictures for her. Sister Rose was very keen on refinement. She inspired us all with the idea of culture, of being "Ladies".

By a word here and a glance there, Sister Rose gave me to understand that Maria was not refined. For a while I was still loyal to Maria, but then I began to see her with Sister Rose's eyes. I forgot her good nature, and only heard the raucous tones of her loud voice. One day as we were both drying our hands together after cookery class I saw Maria's rough red hands against the white towel. Maria had to do most of the work at home because she was the eldest of six children. My own hands were smooth and white like Sister Rose's. I decided to give up Maria for Sister Rose. The next time we were alone together I made my offering: I told Sister Rose that I understood what she had been trying to tell me; I now saw that Maria was a "lower-class" person, and I promised not to associate with her any more because I wanted to do what Sister Rose thought best.

To my surprise, Sister Rose stared at me in horror. She backed away, then made an excuse and left the room. When we returned in the fall we heard that she had left the Order. I never saw Sister Rose again.

I understood the horror on Sister Rose's face when I heard my own children repeating my bad-tempered remarks in exactly my own tone of voice. It was the most terrible lesson; in hearing them I had to become aware of what I was like. On the other hand I found that the more I tried to be aware of my own faults, the more the children were set free. It was a strange kind of inheritance to give them, but the only one which seemed to work. If I tried to point out to them their own shortcomings, they rebelled.

There is a story about Mahatma Gandhi. One day a woman came to him with her little boy and said, "Please tell my son to stop eating sugar". Gandhi told her to bring her son back in three days. When she did Gandhi said to the little boy, "Stop eating sugar". The woman said to Gandhi, "Why couldn't you have told him that three days ago?" "Because at that time," said Gandhi, "I was still eating sugar."

> If you wish your children well, you must first wish yourself well. For if you change, your children too will change. For the sake of their future you must, for a time, forget about them and think about yourself.
>
> If we are satisfied with ourselves, we can continue with

a clear conscience to educate our children as we have done up to now. But are you satisfied with yourselves?

We must always start with ourselves and take ourselves as an example, for we cannot see another man through the mask he wears. Only if we know ourselves can we see others, for all people are alike inside and others are the same as we are. They have the same good intentions to be better, but they cannot be; it is just as hard for them; they are equally unhappy, equally full of regrets afterwards. You must forgive what there is in them now and remember the future. If you are sorry for yourself, then for the sake of the future you must be sorry in advance for others.[9]

18

Nature

One of my earliest memories is going into the garden in the early morning and finding a blue flower as big as my hand. As I gazed at it, it seemed to widen out, and I felt myself swallowed up in a glorious sea of pure blueness.

When I was older I loved to sit in the grass making flower chains; but all the time a great curiosity seized me. At what point did a flower begin? I opened smaller and smaller buds, hoping to discover the origin of life, but I never succeeded in finding it.

At ten years old I went with my family to a summer holiday in the Canadian mountains. Here nature was at her grandest, particularly when autumn came and the woods were on fire with colour. Then the day came when we were to leave and go to live in Montreal. I slipped away early to say goodbye to the mountains. Many of the glowing yellow and orange leaves had fallen, looking like embers on the ground, while the grey bare branches rose above them like smoke. I sat there looking, saying goodbye, and a strange thing happened inside me. Suddenly I knew it was I sitting there, that I was no longer one with nature, thoughtlessly part of her; it was as if I had been thrown out of the nest. From now on I was human and separate, I could look at nature and praise her – I was no longer one with her, as I had been through my childhood.

Praise to the Holy Creator, who has placed his throne upon the waters, and who has made all terrestrial creatures. To the Heavens he has given dominion and to the Earth dependence; to the heavens he has given movement, and to the Earth uniform repose.

He raised the firmament above the earth as a tent, without pillars to uphold it. In six days he created the seven planets and with two letters he created the nine cupolas of the Heavens.

In the beginning he gilded the stars, so that at night the heavens might play tric-trac.

With diverse properties he endowed the net of the body, and he has put dust on the tail of the bird of the soul.

He made the Ocean liquid as a sign of bondage, and the mountain tops are capped with ice for fear of him.

He dried up the bed of the sea, and from its stones brought forth rubies, and from its blood, musk.

To the mountains he has given peaks for a dagger, and valleys for a belt; so that they lift up their heads in pride.

Sun and Moon – one the day, the other the night, bow to the dust in adoration; and from their worship comes their movement. It is God who has spread out the day in whiteness, it is he who has folded up the night and blackened it.

God has made the firmament to revolve – night follows day and day the night.

When he breathes on clay man is created; and from a little vapour he forms the world.

Friends or enemies, all bow the head under the yoke which God, in his wisdom, imposes; and, a thing astonishing, he watches over us all.[1]

We went back to the mountains the following summer, and it was all changed; tractors were there, digging up the trails to make roads, felling trees, and frightening all the wildlife away. I began to suffer from a recurring nightmare, where I would retreat further and further into the forest but the tractors would follow, destroying everything in their path.

In the cities where I was to spend most of my life, there was little chance to live in nature's rhythm, and feel her pulse, as the people of other cultures do. Africans and American Indians have a very special relationship with natural forces, and can perform acts which seem to us miraculous. It is because they understand the flow of forces in the world; that everything connects, everything has to be paid for.

> All life is subject to the "natural law" of the Great Spirit, which is order, balance, and harmony.
>
> We are all held accountable to the same Source, which is truly a "Great Spirit". Those of us who strive for harmony and balance with one another and with the natural way of the Great Spirit are said to walk softly on the earth, to walk on the Red Road . . .
>
> There is more to the Red Road than spoken words or written words on paper. It is behaviour, attitude, a way of living, a way of "doing" with reverence – of walking strong yet softly, so as not to harm or disturb other life. We are stewards, temporarily here to caretake the body we live in and the earth we live on, to fulfil our vision and individual destiny in harmony with one another and in balance with nature.[2]

> Sitting quietly, doing nothing,
> Spring comes, and the grass grows by itself.[3]

Rabbi Bunam was once walking outside the city with some of his disciples. He bent, picked up a speck of sand, looked at it, and put it back exactly where he had found it. "He who does not believe", he said, "that God wants this bit of sand to lie in this particular place, does not believe at all."[4]

A snowflake never falls in the wrong place.[5]

Doug Boyd describes his trip into the countryside with Rolling Thunder, an Indian medicine man. As they are gathering leaves Doug encounters a rattlesnake. Rolling Thunder sees the snake and kneels down in front of it, holding out his hand. The snake raises its head to meet the hand, then does a sort of swaying dance between Rolling Thunder's two outstretched hands. When Rolling Thunder gets up and turns his back, the snake goes limp, then it turns and disappears into the countryside. Doug Boyd writes:

> I had watched Rolling Thunder in dialogue with mosquitoes, ants and now a snake. I believed that when he needed any animal it would be waiting. Rolling Thunder had said that the Earth is an organism, one body of one being. I sensed that Rolling Thunder and the deer, snakes, bees, and mosquitoes, ants and pinyon trees were one being.
>
> Rolling Thunder often wondered out loud why psychiatrists failed to see the causal relationship between mental illness, air and water pollution, and the destruction of forests. Every traditional Indian could see this relationship – this man-mind-nature interaction. Perhaps that is why American Indians are still performing "impossible" agricultural and medical feats; why American Indians are still custodians of the land.
>
> To Rolling Thunder, knowing is being. His simple

> description of the arrangement of the universe is that there is a right time and place for everything . . . Every day in every action, in all his interrelations with the sun, the earth, clouds, mosquitoes, plants, animals and people, he practises the understanding that there is a right time and place for everything. He does not gather herbs after sundown and he only gathers what he needs; he does not take before he gives; he never picks plants to throw them away; he never kills for sport; he never does anything without reason or leaves a thing undone that has a purpose in its doing. For him there are no weeds, no mosquito bites, no unwanted rains. There are no dangerous plants or animals. For him there is no fear. The wind and the rain, the mosquitoes and the snakes are all within him. His consciousness extends to include them within its very being.[6]

In many religions all over the globe, it is emphasized that there is a special link between man and animals. Hindu myths tell of many helpful animal spirits, notably the Garuda bird and Hanuman the monkey. In China the Monkey is a character who attains immortality. Tibetans believe in "Nagas", helpful spirits who appear in animal forms. For the Africans, there is an even closer link:

> "The animal", said Ogotemmêli, "is, as it were, man's twin."
>
> And an ancestor could use the animal which was, so to speak, his twin, to make himself known to the living men whom he wished to help. True, the animal was distinct from him, born elsewhere and to all appearance different in form, but it was of the same essence and was recalled to heaven in the same batch.[7]

In the Bible there is a touching passage in which man is given a very special responsibility towards the animals:

> And out of the ground the Lord God formed every beast of the field, and every fowl of the air; and brought them unto

> Adam to see what he would call them: and whatsoever Adam called every living creature, that was the name thereof. And Adam gave names to all cattle, and to the fowl of the air, and to every beast of the field (Genesis 2:19–20).

I have often pondered on the meaning of the words in Genesis, when God gives Adam the power to name the animals. It seems as if God was calling man to have a special relationship with birds, animals and all living creatures. To name something is to see it with a particular kind of attention, an attention that recognizes and singles out each living being; and appreciates the essence of it. In this moment of seeing and appreciating the creature for what it is, the name arises. The name becomes a recognition, not only for man, the one who names, but also for the one who is named.

In this way it could be said that man's task is to bring a special kind of awareness to the world, to make the world conscious of itself. Jung's experience could stand for us all.

> From a low hill in the Athi plains of East Africa I once watched the vast herds of wild animals grazing in soundless stillness, as they had done from time immemorial, touched only by the breath of a primeval world. I felt then as if I were the first man, the first creature, to know that all this *is*. The entire world round me was still in its primeval state; it did not know that it *was*. And then, in that one moment in which I came to know, the world sprang into being; without that moment it would never have been. All Nature seeks this goal and finds it fulfilled in man, but only in the most highly developed and most fully conscious man.[8]

Because man has the greatest possibility of awareness, it is on him that the responsibility for other beings rests. He was made their custodian.

> Let a man decide upon his favourite animal and make a study of it – let him learn to understand its sounds and motions. The animals want to communicate with man, but Wakan-Tanka does not intend they shall do so directly – man must do the greater part in securing an understanding.[9]

> One should pay attention to even the smallest crawling creature, for these too may have a valuable lesson to teach us, and even the smallest ant may wish to communicate with a man.[10]

There is a truth hidden in all the fables about animals helping man. They are our link with the forces of the earth. These forces exist and more primitive people are aware of them and can work with them. The rituals to do with harvest and sowing are examples of man's early understanding of the interchange of forces.

> All sacrifices . . . have the same effects as the corporate ritual celebrated at the communal sowing. After he has communicated, man speaks, and his Word, impregnated with the virtue of the ancestors, goes out to others.
>
> "The altar gives something to a man, and a part of what he has received he passes on to others", said Ogotemmêli. "A small part of the sacrifice is for oneself, but the rest is for others. The forces released enter into the man, pass through him and out again, and so it is for all . . ." As each man gives to all the rest, so he also receives from all. A perpetual exchange goes on between men, an unceasing movement of invisible currents. And this must be so if the

> universal order is to endure. "The Word", said Ogotemmêli, "is for everyone in this world; it must come and go and be interchanged, for it is good to give and to receive the forces of life."[11]

The giving and receiving of forces, so natural in a primitive ritual, have been disregarded in our Western way of life. But the forces are still there. Man, who was made Lord over the earth, is like a decadent king who shuts himself in his palace, forgetting his subjects, or allowing them to be despoiled, while the army is preparing to overthrow his kingdom. For the forces in Nature are still there, even if we choose not to respect them. Our earth is an organism, just as we are; her health affects our health, we cannot destroy parts of her body without being affected ourselves.

> Rolling Thunder said, "When you have pollution in one place, it spreads all over. It spreads just as arthritis or cancer spreads in the body. The earth is sick now because the earth is being mistreated, and some of the problems that may occur, some of the natural disasters that might happen in the near future, are only the natural readjustments that have to take place to throw off sickness. A lot of things are on this land that don't belong here. They're foreign objects like viruses or germs. Now, we may not recognize the fact when it happens, but a lot of the things that are going to happen in the future will really be the earth's attempt to throw off some of these sicknesses. This is really going to be like fever or like vomiting, what you might call physiological adjustment.
>
> "It's very important for people to realize this. The earth is a living organism, the body of a higher individual who has a will and wants to be well, who is at times less healthy or more healthy, physically and mentally. People should treat their own bodies with respect. It's the same thing with the earth. Too many people don't know that when they

harm the earth they harm themselves, nor do they realize that when they harm themselves they harm the earth . . .

"It's not very easy for you people to understand these things because understanding is not knowing the kind of facts that your books and teachers talk about. I can tell you that understanding begins with love and respect. It begins with respect for the Great Spirit, and the Great Spirit is the life that is in all things – all the creatures and the plants and even the rocks and the minerals. All things – and I mean *all* things – have their own will and their own way and their own purpose; this is what is to be respected.

"Such respect is not a feeling or an attitude only. It's a way of life. Such respect means that we never stop realizing and never neglect to carry out our obligation to ourselves and our environment."[12]

Today we all stand at a cross-roads; we are either at the brink of destruction or on the first step of a conscious choice in favour of trying again to rebuild our world.

What will push us over the brink into destruction, is the failure to understand the power of the spiritual forces in the world. We abuse the earth at our peril:

The daemonism of nature, which man had apparently triumphed over, he has unwittingly swallowed into himself and so become the devil's marionette. This could happen only because he believed he had abolished the daemons by declaring them to be superstition. He overlooked the fact that they were, at bottom, the products of certain factors in the human psyche. When these products were dubbed unreal and illusory, their sources were in no way blocked up or rendered inoperative. On the contrary, after it became impossible for the daemons to inhabit the rocks, woods, mountains, and rivers, they used human beings as much more dangerous dwelling places.[13]

Conversely, we know, most of us, the healing power in Nature. So often we can go out for a walk with a troubled mind, but the countryside will restore us.

One occasion particularly I remember, when I was suffering under a terrible blow; my child had died. I walked along the roads, not able to be alone with my grief. Then I saw a magnolia tree. Its buds were just opening, like candles. It simply stood there, being itself, contained and beautiful, and through that my grief somehow became contained too.

Later, when I read Viktor Frankl's account of a woman in a concentration camp, I was reminded of my own experience.

> This young woman knew that she would die in the next few days. But when I talked to her she was cheerful in spite of this knowledge. "I am grateful that fate has hit me so hard", she told me. "In my former life I was spoiled and did not take spiritual accomplishments seriously." Pointing through the window of the hut, she said, "This tree here is the only friend I have in my loneliness". Through that window she could see just one branch of a chestnut tree, and on the branch were two blossoms. "I often talk to this tree", she said to me. I was startled and didn't quite know how to take her words. Was she delirious? Did she have occasional hallucinations? Anxiously I asked her if the tree replied. "Yes." What did it say to her? She answered, "It said to me, 'I am here – I am here – I am life, eternal life'."[14]

To love and care for the earth – this brings me back again to myself; to my responsibility to become a worthy inhabitant of this world. I wish to become aware of my planet, and its needs.

On man, however, a new and unprecedented law is enjoined: to fulfil what was promised in his nature by inclining himself to all things, and enveloping them in love where and whenever he meets them; in a love that does not reckon and calculate, but squanders itself and only grows richer and deeper in the squandering. Only in this way can he succeed in freeing himself, step by step, from the narrow prison of individuality in which he, like the animals and plants, is confined. In the end he is restored to himself as what he really is: as the heart of existence, in which Being is made manifest.

Reverence for all life is the formula of Zen Buddhism, and in this is hidden the secret of Zen.[15]

We should understand well that all things are the works of the Great Spirit. We should know that He is within all things: the trees, the grasses, the rivers, the mountains, and all the four-legged animals, and the winged peoples; and even more important, we should understand that He is also above all these things and peoples. When we do understand all this deeply in our hearts, then we will fear, and love, and know the Great Spirit, and then we will be and act and live as He intends.[16]

The earth is my mother, the earth is my mother,
She will take care of me.
The earth is my mother, the earth is my mother,
I will take care of her.[17]

19

Death

Although in the past it used to be considered as a natural part of life, we in the West have become very squeamish about death. Still, as we shall all have to undergo the experience, it would seem more profitable to think about it. The Tibetans rather disconcertingly make many of their religious objects from human bones: masks from human skulls, flutes from thigh-bones, etc. When I was in a Tibetan monastery and asked about it, the head monk answered, with a twinkle in his eye, that this was done to remind them of impermanence. It worked, too. I couldn't live there for long without thinking seriously about the fact of my own death.

Most of us are afraid of death, and with good reason. I used to be terrified at the thought of death when I was a child, and I wasn't much better as I got older. It wasn't just the fear of a painful death, although that wasn't absent, but it was the horror of being snuffed out, of not existing . . . Even when, as a believer, I accepted that I would exist in some form, not knowing what form my existence would take terrified me. I had a sneaking feeling that once I was stripped of my body, there mightn't be much soul left!

But fear doesn't help; what will happen, will happen. Therefore my fear has no place, or only a place as a spur to practise meditation. In meditation my emotions are all resolved in the inner quietness and acceptance.

Herrigel tells a story from the "Hagakure" of the great swordsman and teacher of the seventeenth century, Tajima-no-kami. One day a man came to him for training in fencing. The master said, "I saw you fencing just now, and you seem to be a master yourself; where did you train?"

The man answered, "I am ashamed to confess that I have never been trained."

The master insisted that the man must have been trained somewhere, saying, "My judging eye never fails."

The man insisted again that he had never been instructed, until the master swordsman thought it over, and said finally, "Well then, you must be a master of something!"

The man answered:

> "If you insist, I will tell you. There is one thing of which I can say I am complete master. When I was still a boy, the thought came upon me that as a Samurai I ought in no circumstances to be afraid of death, and I have grappled with the problem of death now for some years, and finally the problem of death ceased to worry me. May this be at what you hint?"
>
> "Exactly!" exclaimed Tajima-no-kami. "That is what I mean. I am glad that I made no mistake in my judgement. For the ultimate secrets of swordsmanship also lie in being released from the thought of death."[1]

In *Journey to Ixtlan* by Carlos Castenada, Don Juan speaks to Castenada about the value of realizing that he is going to die. In the light of his own death, he would no longer be interested in giving vent to his temper, or sulking.

> "Focus your attention on the fact you don't have time and let your acts flow accordingly. Let each of your acts be your last battle on earth. Only under those conditions will your acts have their rightful power. Otherwise they will be, for as long as you live, the acts of a timid man."
>
> "Is it so terrible to be a timid man?"
>
> "No. It isn't if you are going to be immortal, but if you are going to die there is no time for timidity, simply because timidity makes you cling to something that exists only in

your thoughts. It soothes you while everything is at a lull, but then the awesome, mysterious world will open its mouth for you, as it will open for every one of us, and then you will realize that your sure ways were not sure at all. Being timid prevents us from examining and exploiting our lot as men. . . .

"A hunter, on the contrary, assesses every act; and since he has an intimate knowledge of his death, he proceeds judiciously, as if every act were his last battle. Only a fool would fail to notice the advantage a hunter has over his fellow men. A hunter gives his last battle its due respect. It's only natural that his last act on earth should be the best of himself. It's pleasurable that way. It dulls the edge of his fright."[2]

Ram Dass writes of his visit to "death row" in San Quentin prison, the place where criminals under the death penalty are kept. Those men were in separate cells, segregated by a wall.

As I went up to each cell, out of the thirty-four men, there were not more than five who did not receive me openly, clearly, quietly, consciously. The feeling I had was that I was visiting a monastery and that these were monks in their cells. For these men, who are facing death, have been pushed into a situation that has cut through their melodrama and they are right here. We sat together in groups of ten and as part of the meditation we are sending out through forms of love and peace to all sentient beings in the universe. I became so affected by the vibration of the space that it was very hard for me to move on to the next group. There was light pouring out of these beings' eyes.

And we got so open that I was able to say . . . "I can't tell whether what's happened to you is a blessing or a curse, for there is very little chance that we would be sharing this high a space or even would have met were you not in this situation." To prove my point, I'll tell you that I spent half an hour on one of the other segregated main-line

> cell-blocks. And of these beings the percentage of those open were just what you'd expect in our society . . . you could feel the cynicism, the doubt, the put-down, the sarcasm.[3]

> The birth of a human being is pregnant with meaning, why not death? For twenty years and more the growing man is being prepared for the complete unfolding of his individual nature, why should not the older man prepare himself twenty years and more for his death? . . .
>
> As a doctor I am convinced that it is hygienic – if I may use the word – to discover in death a goal towards which one can strive, and that shrinking away from it is something unhealthy and abnormal which robs the second half of life of its purpose.[4]

It is a very sad thing for dying people in our culture that we find death a difficult and even embarrassing situation, because the dying person feels rejected by society. This is not so in other cultures. In the Tibetan tradition people often gather near to be with the dying person and pray and meditate in the same room, so that these prayers can assist the one who is dying through his death more easily, and his soul to the highest place in the realms of the world of the spirit.

Chogyam Trungpa says that it is important for the person to be told that he is going to die:

> It seems necessary, unless the dying person is in a coma or cannot communicate, that he should be told he is dying. It may be difficult to actually take such a step, but if one is a friend or a husband or wife, then this is the greatest opportunity of really communicating trust. It is a delightful situation, that at last somebody really cares about you, somebody is not playing a game of hypocrisy, is not going to tell you a lie in order to please you, which is what has been happening throughout your whole life. This comes down to the ultimate truth, it is fundamental trust, which

> is extremely beautiful. We should really try to generate that principle.
>
> Actually relating with the dying person is very important, telling him that death is not a myth at that point, but that it is actually happening. "It is actually happening, but we are your friends, therefore we are watching your death. We know that you are dying and you know that you are dying, we are really meeting together at this point." That is the finest and best demonstration of friendship and communication, it presents tremendously rich inspiration to the dying person.[5]

I was twice called in to hospital to see my son after he had taken an overdose. The first time he was in intensive care, he was in a deep coma, but he lived through it. He looked very peaceful and beautiful lying there. On the second occasion, he was dead, and I had to identify his body. They lifted a sheet, and what I saw was that my son was no longer there. What lay there was something that looked as if it had been made of clay. I knew then instantly that wherever my son had gone he was not in the empty shell in front of me.

The death of someone close is a profound shock. I felt as if my whole life had been a film, that someone had come with scissors and cut it off, and that I was left with a great blank. Then it seemed I had only one choice; to say "Yes" or "No" to life. I chose to say "Yes".

> If we kept the searchlight of our observation turned upon the fact of death, the world would appear to us like a huge charnel-house; but in the world of life the thought of death has, we find, the least possible hold upon our minds. Not because it is the least apparent, but because it is the negative aspect of life; just as, in spite of the fact that we shut our eyelids every second, it is the openings of the eyes that count. Life as a whole never takes death seriously. It laughs, dances and plays, it builds, hoards and loves in

death's face. Only when we detach one individual fact of death do we see its blankness and become dismayed.[6]

Man is born with his hands clenched; he dies with his hands wide open. Entering life he desires to grasp everything; leaving the world, all that he possessed has slipped away.

Even as a fox is man; as a fox which seeing a fine vineyard lusted after its grapes. But the palings were placed at narrow distances, and the fox was too bulky to creep between them. For three days he fasted, and when he had grown thin he entered into the vineyard. He feasted upon the grapes, forgetful of the morrow, of all things but his enjoyment; and lo, he had again grown stout and was unable to leave the scene of his feast. So for three days more he fasted, and when he had again grown thin, he passed through the palings and stood outside the vineyard, meagre as when he entered.

So with man; poor and naked he enters the world, poor and naked does he leave.[7]

I found that the ceremony connected with my son's funeral was very helpful to me at the time. The order of the ritual seemed to uphold the order of life against the terrible disorder of death. The fact that at this occasion all my family and friends gathered together around me gave me strength; and choosing the readings for the church service was a comfort. Because my son's life had had so much suffering in it, I chose the words from St John's gospel which promise: "God shall wipe away all tears from their eyes."

In other religions many such helpful rituals have been handed down. In a Zen Buddhist monastery in San Francisco, I was present at a vigil being kept for a member of the community who had died. A group of monks sat in prayer for the soul of the one who had departed. Quietly a few would slip away from time to time, and a few would come in. In that way the vigil was maintained for three days. It seemed so right that this soul, embarking on its voyage out into the unknown spirit world, should be attended by the outpouring of the prayers and good thoughts of his friends.

Gurdjieff describes a funeral ceremony from ancient times, when it was the custom for friends and relatives to meet together after the death of someone, and contemplate the inevitability of their own death. They recalled the times when the departed man had behaved unworthily, because he had not accepted the fact that he was going to die, and then they prayed to the Higher Forces that they themselves might always keep death before their eyes, so as not to succumb to temptation.

> "It would be desirable for all, for God, for the deceased, for you, for me and even for the whole of humanity, if, at the death of any person, instead of the process of the expression of senseless words, the process of the real grasping of your own forthcoming death would take place in you.
>
> "Only the complete realization by man of the inevitability of his own death can destroy those factors, implanted thanks to our abnormal life, of the expression of different aspects of our egoism, this cause of all evil in our common life.
>
> "Only such a realization can bring to birth again in man those formerly present, divine proofs of genuine impulses – faith, love and hope."[8]

20

East and West

After studying Eastern spiritual thought for so many years, I wanted to visit some Eastern religious centres. I went to Japan, Indonesia and India, meeting some very fine people. However, what I wanted most of all was to see a Tibetan Buddhist monastery, and perhaps be fortunate enough to get an audience with a Rinpoche or Tibetan teacher. The Chinese had broken up the monasteries in Tibet and disbanded the monks, so it was no use going there, but I heard that in Ladakh, in the Himalayas, the monastic life of the Tibetan Buddhists continued undisturbed. It is not easy to get there; because of the great altitude it is inadvisable to fly in, as you need to get accustomed to it gradually. The trip overland from Srinagar was very uncomfortable. It took two days in a jeep over high mountains with dizzying hair-pin bends, and a driver who had a disconcerting habit of driving on the extreme edge of the cliff the whole time. I arrived in a very spiritual frame of mind, having consigned my soul several times to my Maker!

When I finally got to Leh and began to visit the monasteries nearby, I was disappointed. By that time there were tourists in Ladakh, and as they came often to the monasteries there were monks to serve as guides and charge admittance, but no chance of speaking with one of the Rinpoches.

An Englishwoman who had come out to Ladakh to start a school befriended me. She told me that in one of the more remote monasteries lived the Rinpoche of Ladakh, and it might be possible to get an audience with him. An added advantage was that he spoke English.

I set out over rough roads, and stayed in a tiny guest-house, at the foot of the monastery, overlooking the Himalayan mountains. There a young monk called Tashi came and spoke with me. I told him that I would like an audience with the Rinpoche, whom Tashi called His Holiness. The days passed, and to my chagrin two visitors who had not asked were given an audience, while I was passed over. I became upset and jealous, until I began to see how my greed was spoiling life for me. Why not give up my wishes and be content with being there in these beautiful surroundings? I started a painting of the scene from my window, and peace flooded me.

On my last morning there I saw Tashi come running down the slope towards me, a beaming smile on his face. His Holiness had granted me an audience! A visitor had just arrived, an Austrian named Josef who looked on enviously, so I asked Tashi if Josef could come too. Tashi nodded, and we followed him up the steep slope and through the various levels in the monastery until we came to a hidden sanctuary, where Tashi left us. We sat down quietly, trying to prepare ourselves, and to find questions that were worthy of the occasion.

A different monk came out of a dark hallway, and beckoned us in. We took off our shoes and were given white scarves. Silently the monk drew aside a heavy curtain and we went into a room filled with colour and light.

At the far end of the room sat a man looking exactly like a statue of Buddha. His large well-shaped head was shaved, and he wore robes of a deep rose-pink, richly colourful against his bronzed skin. There was a strength emanating from him. It made me think of the vibrations from a powerful electricity generator. As we entered he stood up to greet us. Timidly I walked forward holding the white scarf, not knowing what to do with it. I gave an awkward bow as I got to him and held out the scarf. He took it with a smile in his expressive dark eyes, put it round his shoulders for a moment and then placed it round my neck, with the affectionate gesture of a mother dressing her child for going outdoors. He beckoned us both to a low couch with a little table in front, holding tea, fruit and biscuits, great luxuries in this part of the world. Then he sat down and waited for us to speak.

Josef said, "Your Holiness, tell me please, is there any hope for the world?"

The Rinpoche thought for a moment, then he said very seriously, "If there is love and compassion among men, then yes, there is hope, but if everyone is egoistic, then there is no hope."

"But how can we increase love and compassion?" I asked urgently.

He turned his dark eyes on me. "Meditate", he said. "If you meditate, love and compassion are given."

Josef asked again, "Is the world getting better or worse?"

The Rinpoche seemed to consider within himself for some moments. Then he said, "I think the world is getting better. I think love and compassion are increasing."

Josef burst out suddenly, "Your Holiness, I have travelled all over the world and visited many places, churches and cathedrals even; but never have I experienced such peace as in this room. How do you do it?"

His words fell upon a great wall of silence. It was an awkward moment. Then I asked His Holiness to tell us something of his life.

"I heard that you were trained in Tibet", I added.

He answered that he had been born in Ladakh, had been discovered by a delegation of lamas from Tibet to be an Incarnation at the age of three, and had been carried in state to a large monastery in Tibet, where he had been in training when the Chinese had invaded. They disbanded the monastery, and his relatives had fled to America, but he had been held hostage at fourteen, and his training as a monk had ended. Four years later he managed to escape, and was smuggled over the border into Nepal. From there he had gone to America to see his relatives; then he came back to Dharamsala, where the Dalai Lama was based, and finished his training as a monk.

I was interested to hear that he had been to America. "What were your first impressions when you got there?" I asked.

The Rinpoche smiled. "In Tibet, in China, you must always be so careful, always watching so as not to get into trouble. In America everyone is so free – doing what they want all the time. It seemed to me like a jungle!"

"But what did you do in America?" Josef asked. "How did you live?"

The Rinpoche's smile broadened. "I got a job," he said, "I worked in McDonald's!"

Josef's jaw dropped. "What if one of your monks had seen you!" he exclaimed.

But I thought to myself how strange it was to come all this way to the most remote and inaccessible place, and still find someone who had worked in McDonald's! It seemed clear that nothing could prevent the mixing of East and West! If only we could take the best from each other, and not the worst.

One thing we in the West have lost touch with is the idea of magic. In the East, magic is part of the everyday life of people, but the Western scientific mind is made uneasy by the thought of it, and yet we are intrigued and puzzled by the thought that there might be a force that seems to break the laws of the material world.

In the beginning of my travels one of the most fascinating ideas to me about the East was the thought that I might get to see real magic. In fact I did. In Bali I saw a man dancing barefoot on fiery coals, and two little girls dancing in unison under hypnosis; but the strangest experiences were in Ladakh, where a Tibetan Oracle stuck swords into himself without any wounds or bleeding, and later smashed a huge stone boulder on to the naked stomach of a man in a loincloth. The man ought to have been killed, but instead the boulder smashed into very tiny pieces.

Later I asked Chospel, the owner of the guesthouse where I was staying, "How was this done? Did the man make his stomach hard?" "Other man not do any magic," he told me, "only Oracle. To make this ceremony he must fast and meditate three months. Then he makes the stone light."

It was fascinating to hear about, but I found that I didn't enjoy experiencing magic as much as I thought I would. For some reason I felt a strange fear and nausea while it was taking place.

Nevertheless, I knew that magic was not so far away from all of us in the West. During times of stress people often have second sight or foretell the future. There is more of the supernatural around us than we are usually prepared to admit.

After the audience with His Holiness was over, and I had returned to Leh, I thought of other questions that I would have liked to ask the Rinpoche, but now there was no chance, or so I thought. But fate had a surprise in store for me.

When I boarded the plane from Leh on my homeward journey, to my delight, His Holiness the Rinpoche of Ladakh was on the plane too. He indicated that I could sit in the empty seat beside him, and I was able to put more questions to him about the things which had been puzzling me, mainly about the place that magic had in the Buddhist faith. The Rinpoche smiled. He said that magic had very little place in Buddhism. He felt that much of it was a kind of hypnotism. However, he accepted that there was such a thing as magic, but it should not be seen as an end in itself. The real magic was connected with inner work.

As he spoke I was reminded of a story, about a man who wanted to learn magic. He went to a yogi and asked him if he could teach him to read thoughts. The yogi advised the merchant to start by spending three nights at a little hut. The merchant did so and came back to the yogi looking tired and miserable. "What happened?" asked the yogi. The merchant said that he hadn't been able to sleep because two drunkards next door were shouting at each other all the time.

> "Yes, I heard all this in passing when I first came here", said the yogi. "But you did know their thoughts, didn't you? They were shouting them. I wanted you to have that experience – that's what it would be like. Voices yelling in your head all the time."
>
> "Surely one could learn to switch off the telepathy by mental control, couldn't one?" asked the merchant. "Then it would do one no harm."
>
> "That is true. So you could begin now practising how to withdraw your attention from external disturbances; it will help you to make real spiritual progress. But when you can spend three days and nights in that hut without being disturbed, switching off your attention by mental control, then if you like I will teach you telepathy. It may take you quite a few years."
>
> The merchant thought for a bit, and then laughed.
>
> "Tell me about real spiritual progress," he asked, "not this stuff."[1]

I began to see that, just as religions can be on many levels, so magic is on many levels. There is the startling kind that tourists come to gape at; and there is the more subtle magic that performs an inner miracle, where one is guided mysteriously, and helped to become more sensitive to the spiritual forces at work around us.

Jacob Needleman, in his book *Lost Christianity*, speaks of the necessity for paying less attention to the outward forms of religion and instead trying to find a greater sensitivity to the forces of the spirit. Magic for him is the working of those forces inside us.

> Without magic, without inner results that can be sensed, man loses the sense of wonder before the Creation that is within himself, the movement up and down of his own inner energies. Only this self-knowledge can generate real

> compassion for my neighbour and real knowledge of him and a true sense of justice toward him. Those who love justice without long experience of these inner forces will never bring about anything but more violence and hatred.[2]

Spiritual energy, magic of the highest kind, is a higher level of force. The ability to see and discriminate between levels of energies is at the heart of all religious teachings.

> Sensitivity to qualities of energy is the one and only touchstone for determining the level or authenticity of Christian practices. The discipline, way of living, ideas, practices, that enable a man to acquire this sensitivity in the whole of himself stands as the esoteric tradition at the heart of every revelation. Only there may one speak of the unity of all man's religions. Every other attempt to identify similarities among traditions is false ecumenism.
>
> On both the individual and collective levels, the Spirit does result in attainments in all the realms of human life – mind, social forms, culture, an enduring sense of personal worth and the normal psychological comfort which accompanies it. Spiritual energy can and must descend, as God's grace, into these forms of goodness on earth – such is the nature of God's power and "magic".[3]

However, when the forms of goodness through which God has given us His energy are repeated beyond their term, and without understanding the causal energy behind them, they degenerate into lower forms – superstition, or magic on a lower level, without religion.

In order to work towards receiving higher energies, religious discipline can awaken my spiritual emotion. But for this sacrifice is necessary.

> The sacrifice of what? What is the inner purpose of sacrifice? I must sacrifice attachment to results of the spirit – *even as they are taking place in me*. Religious man may become

> a magician, but through becoming such he sees only the greatness of God and the insignificance of his own being. The energies of egoistic emotion, the psychic and mechanical energies, that, through the inherent structure of human nature, are bound to his inner or outer results are immediately separated from these results and are transformed upward and therewith connected to the Tree of Life, the conduit of the power of God. Thus sacrifice brings union with God. Without this understanding, both self-indulgence and asceticism are equivalently inhuman.[4]

This magic, this spiritual energy, knows no boundaries. Like the faith of the level of water, or the faith of the level of air, it penetrates everywhere, from East to West.

Entering into Oriental spiritual thought can bring one back renewed to one's own faith. One of the characters in Andrew Harvey's book on Ladakh expresses this very well.

> "The West and East are not finally separated. I can speak of what I know – that my love of Eastern thought has helped me to read Western thought and philosophy with a new mind. . . . There is so much in our own tradition that is hidden from us. How few read the Western mystics – Eckhart and St John and Teresa. I have read very little serious modern writing about the relations between spirituality and creativity that have been the inspiration for most of the geniuses of Western art. Almost immediately after I had returned that first time from Dharamsala, I went on a kind of pilgrimage through Europe to visit the great European cathedrals, Chartres, Canterbury, Rheims . . . and as I did so I realized with growing desperation and anger that what we have been most deprived of, as Westerners brought up in a materialistic age, is the richest, most spiritual part of our own culture . . . And it was coming out East that helped me to see that, to become aware of that . . .
>
> I know now that there is a dialogue possible between the truths of East and West, a dialogue of extraordinary beauty

> and complexity. Perhaps, from that dialogue, which we are only just beginning, will come truths as yet unformed and unglimpsed by either East or West, truths that may, in some way none of us can foresee, fuse the dynamic intuitions and practice of Western philosophy and science and the transcendental insight of the East. Sometimes, when I am in despair, I think that to pursue this dialogue seriously is the last hope for the West to listen not merely to Eastern voices, but to its own buried and banished voices, the voices it has silenced at its peril – the voices of Plato, of Dante, of Eckhart – all those voices that speak of ecstasy and the long labour of the spirit.[5]

Gurdjieff, as early as the 1920s, predicted the rise of the East to a position of world importance. He said that one should look at the world in the same way as one looked at an individual. What was important was to find a way in which the two sides of man, and the two sides of the earth, could live together in harmony.

Philosophy, religions, politics, in so far as they treated man in the mass, had failed. The only way to achieve this harmony and peace was the growth of the individual.

He warned us that time was short. It was necessary to achieve this harmony as soon as possible to avoid complete disaster.

> As an individual developed his own, unknown potentialities, he would become strong and would, in turn, influence many more people. If enough individuals could develop themselves – even partially – into genuine, natural men, able to use the real potentialities that were proper to mankind, each such individual would then be able to convince and win over as many as a hundred other men who would, each in his turn, upon achieving development, be able to influence another hundred, and so on . . . the separate, distinct growth of each individual in the world was the only possible solution.[6]

We are brought back again to our own personal development – our work on ourselves.

Krishnamurti gave a vivid example of how the development of the individual can help all those surrounding him or her; by making use of an analogy with an experiment on rats!

Some scientists had put some rats in a tank of water with two outlets, one dark and one light. When a rat chose the light outlet it was given an electric shock; after several attempts, it chose the dark outlet and escaped. The parent rats took a long time to discover this but their children learned much more quickly.

They carried out this experiment in England, Australia and America, and found that when there was one rat which learned more quickly, that quickness was transferred to the whole consciousness of all the rats.

> And if you as a human being recognize that you are the whole of humanity and that therefore you are extraordinarily responsible – without any feeling of guilt – then your consciousness undergoes a change, obviously . . . if you transform yourself through the liberation of insight, you are communicating it to the whole consciousness of man. This happens – the great rulers of the world, or the great killers of the world, have affected the human mind, Attila, Genghis Khan, Napoleon, Hitler, and on the other side Buddha and others. They have all affected the human mind, human consciousness. But if we actually, daily live with this intelligence, the insight which liberates, then we are bringing to the whole of the consciousness of man a totally different value, a different movement which is not based on knowledge. It is based on insight and intelligence.[7]

So how can I be transformed? How can I find the magical spiritual energies that could help me?

> To have any chance of reaching his aim without going astray or getting lost, a man needs a guide for the study of himself. Here as elsewhere, he must learn from those who

> know, and accept to be guided by those who have already trodden the same path . . . It cannot be found in books, which can give only theoretical data, mere information, leaving the whole of the real work still to be done – transforming the information into understanding, and then the understanding into self-knowledge.[8]

In the East, a spiritual teacher is regarded as an essential part of any development towards spiritual growth. It is felt that there is something in ourselves that can easily go off in the wrong direction; someone who has already gone ahead and knows the path, can help us to keep on the right track.

> "There are as many Ways as there are souls of men", said the Murshid, while he was waiting for me to reply.
>
> I asked him who were the real teachers, and how one could tell who was a real teacher.
>
> "A sugar-loaf you weigh against a weight, or against another sugar-loaf", he said, with a laugh. "A teacher you cannot weigh against another teacher. You have to weigh him against yourself. Now comes your problem: when you are weighing a teacher you are not weighing an inert thing. He can, if he desires, increase or decrease his weight. Do you understand me?"
>
> "Do you mean that the teacher has to accept me before I can judge him?"
>
> "It is something as difficult as that. You see, you cannot choose your teacher by logic. The reason is that logic does not extend into the field in which the teacher is operating. This is why it is better for the teacher to choose you."
>
> ". . . The would-be disciple approaches the potential teacher and opens his heart to him. This means that he allows himself to become receptive to what the teacher is *saying and doing*. He must absorb something of the whole entity, the wholeness, the personage of the teacher *and his works*. Then a contact can be made. There is a recognition in the mind of the disciple that this is the teacher for him.

If the recognition is false, the teacher will send him packing."

"Then how does the disciple know when he is following a true teacher?"

"Because something has happened to him, inside. This something is reflected in everything which he does. He is not the same man after the regeneration is accomplished. The change in the social powers and the material achievements of the disciple are obvious to everyone: obvious to the complete outsider, who always remarks upon it. A man is attracted to a teacher of the degree of sincerity which he has himself attained."[9]

There is a saying in the East that "When the pupil is ready the master will appear".

Fourteen years ago I met and began to study with a man who had himself been a pupil of Gurdjieff. In this way I felt from within the value of the pupil-teacher relationship for spiritual growth. I found that there was often a blind spot in myself – I needed to be shown from someone outside myself where I was veering in the wrong direction. This man was able to understand me, and the direction towards which I wanted to go; he was able to pull me up when I got despondent, and give me a gentle (or not so gentle) rap when I became over-weening.

In this way my reading became fleshed out, it became more possible to incorporate what my mind had grasped into my whole life. I was helped in my efforts to try to live my own faith in a new and deeper way towards becoming a truer Christian.

Sometimes when watching the news on television, or reading the paper, I feel driven to despair by the way men seem bent on destroying each other. At such times I have said, "I feel bad about this, but what can one person do?"

Now I can't say that any more. It seems that it is *only* one person who can do anything. But I think, "Why me? I'm not a saint, when I look inside I see that I'm pretty mediocre – what have I got to give?"

Then the words of His Holiness, the Rinpoche of Ladakh, come back to me: "If you meditate, Love and Compassion are given."

I am still.
I listen and see the silence.
I listen and embrace the silence.
I enter into the great silence.
Though hidden, Grandfather dwells in all.[10]

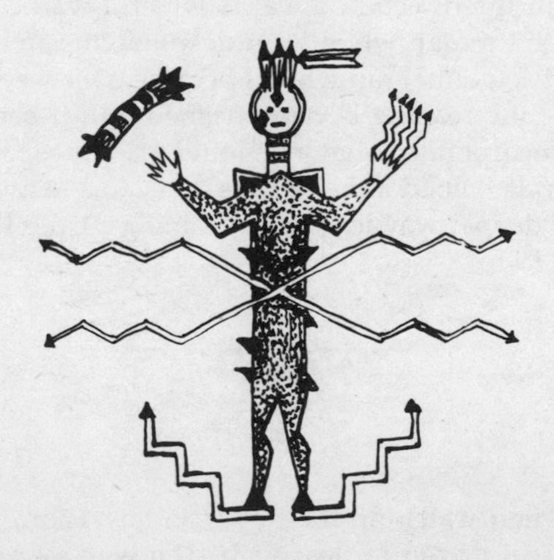

O lovers, O lovers, it is time to abandon the world;
The drum of departure reaches my spiritual ear from heaven.
Behold, the driver has risen and made ready the file of camels,
And begged us to acquit him of blame: why, O travellers, are you asleep?
These sounds before and behind are the din of departure and of the camel-bells;
With each moment a soul and a spirit is setting off into the void.
From these stars like inverted candles, from these blue awnings of the sky
There has come forth a wondrous people, that the mysteries may be revealed.
A heavy slumber fell upon thee from the circling spheres:
Alas for this life so light, beware of this slumber so heavy!
O soul, seek the Beloved, O friend, seek the Friend,
O watchman, be wakeful: it behoves not a watchman to sleep.
On every side is clamour and tumult, in every street are torches and candles,
For tonight the teeming world gives birth to the world everlasting.
Thou wert dust and art a spirit, thou wert ignorant and art wise.[11]

Notes

CHAPTER ONE

1. C. G. Jung, *Psychological Reflections*, Ark Paperbacks
2. Hasidic saying
3. Chogyam Trungpa, *Cutting Through Spiritual Materialism*, Shambala 1973
4. Louis Brenner, *West African Sufi*, C. Hurst & Co. 1984
5. P. D. Ouspensky, *In Search of the Miraculous*, Harcourt, Brace & World 1949
6. Jean Vaysse, *Towards Awakening*, Routledge & Kegan Paul 1980
7. Lao Tzu, *Tao Te Ching*, translated by D. C. Lau, Penguin Books 1963
8. A. J. Arberry, *Muslim Saints and Mystics*, Persian Heritage series: Routledge & Kegan Paul
9. Persian saying

CHAPTER TWO

1. C. G. Jung, *Psychological Reflections*, Ark Paperbacks
2. René Daumal, *A Night of Serious Drinking*, Routledge & Kegan Paul 1979
3. P. D. Ouspensky, *In Search of the Miraculous*, Harcourt, Brace & World 1949
4. ibid.
5. Gotama Buddha, 563–483 B.C.
6. Tsangyang Gyatso in *Tibetan Folk Tales* by F. and A. Hyde-Chambers, Shambala 1981
7. G. I. Gurdjieff, *Meetings with Remarkable Men*, Arkana: Routledge & Kegan Paul 1963

8. ibid.
9. Martin Buber, *Good and Evil*, Charles Scribner's Sons 1952

CHAPTER THREE

1. C. G. Jung, *Psychological Reflections*, Ark Paperbacks
2. ibid.
3. Maurice Nicoll, *Psychological Commentaries on the Teaching of Gurdjieff and Ouspensky*, Shambala
4. ibid.
5. Martin Buber, *The Way of Man*, Routledge & Kegan Paul
6. Cecil Lewis, *A Way To Be*, Fount Paperbacks 1977 and Fine Books Oriental 1984
7. Chogyam Trungpa, *Cutting Through Spiritual Materialism*, Shambala 1973
8. Martin Buber, *Between Man and Man*, Collins
9. Martin Buber, *The Way of Man*, Routledge & Kegan Paul
10. *The Bhagavad-Gita*

CHAPTER FOUR

1. Martin Buber, *Ten Rungs: Hasidic Sayings*, Schocken Books
2. C. G. Jung, *Psychological Reflections*, Ark Paperbacks
3. The Avesta
4. Laurens van der Post, *Jung and the Story of Our Time*, The Hogarth Press 1976
5. C. G. Jung, ibid.
6. Martin Buber, *Good and Evil*, Charles Scribner's Sons 1952
7. Cecil Lewis, *A Way To Be*, Fount Paperbacks 1977 and Fine Books Oriental 1984
8. Chogyam Trungpa, *Journey Without Goal*, Prajna Press
9. C. G. Jung, ibid.
10. Chogyam Trungpa, *Meditation in Action*, Watkins Publishers 1969
11. J. Krishnamurti, Brockwood Park Lecture, September 1981, Krishnamurti Foundation Trust
12. Chogyam Trungpa, *Cutting Through Spiritual Materialism*, Shambala 1973
13. Martin Buber, *Ten Rungs: Hasidic Sayings*, Shocken Books

CHAPTER FIVE

1. Idries Shah, *The Exploits of the Incomparable Mulla Nasrudin*, Octagon Press 1985
2. J. Krishnamurti, *Commentaries on Living*, Krishnamurti Writings Inc., Garden City Press 1956
3. O. M. Burke, *Among the Dervishes*, E. P. Dutton 1973
4. Martin Buber, *Between Man and Man*, Collins
5. Dom Aelred Graham, *Zen Catholicism*, Catholic Book Club
6. C. G. Jung, *Psychological Reflections*, Ark Paperbacks
7. P. D. Ouspensky, *In Search of the Miraculous*, Harcourt, Brace & World 1949
8. A. J. Arberry, *The Discourses of Rumi*, John Murray 1961
9. Simone Weil, *Waiting on God*, Routledge & Kegan Paul 1951 and Fount Paperbacks 1959

CHAPTER SIX

1. Chogyam Trungpa, *The Myth of Freedom and the Way of Meditation*, Shambala 1976
2. idem
3. Idries Shah, *The Wisdom of the Idiots*, Octagon Press 1969
4. P. D. Ouspensky, *In Search of the Miraculous*, Harcourt, Brace & World 1949
5. C. G. Jung, *Psychological Reflections*, Ark Publications
6. Shunryu Suzuki, *Zen Mind, Beginner's Mind*, John Weatherhill Inc. 1970
7. René Daumal, *Mount Analogue*, Vincent Stuart

CHAPTER SEVEN

1. Chogyam Trungpa, *Cutting Through Spiritual Materialism*, Shambala 1973
2. idem
3. Fritz Peters, *Boyhood with Gurdjieff*, E. P. Dutton and Wildwood House 1964
4. A. R. Orage, *On Love*, Samuel Weiser, Janus Press 1974
5. idem
6. idem
7. Viktor Frankl, *Man's Search for Meaning – Experiences in a*

Concentration Camp, Beacon Press 1959; originally *From Death Camp to Existentialism*, Hodder & Stoughton 1962

8. idem
9. Ösel Tendzin, *Buddha in the Palm of Your Hand*, Shambala 1982

CHAPTER EIGHT

1. Luis S. R. Vas, *The Mind of J. Krishnamurti*, Jaico Publishing House 1973
2. A. J. Arberry, *The Discourses of Rumi*, John Murray 1961
3. C. G. Jung, *Psychological Reflections*, Ark Paperbacks
4. Doug Boyd, *Rolling Thunder*, Delta Books
5. C. S. Nott, *The Teachings of Gurdjieff – A Journal of a Pupil*, Routledge & Kegan Paul 1961
6. Hermann Hesse, *Autobiographical Writings*, Jonathan Cape 1973 and Pan Books

CHAPTER NINE

1. Eugen Herrigel, *The Method of Zen*, Routledge & Kegan Paul 1980
2. ibid.
3. Doug Boyd, *Rolling Thunder*, Delta Books
4. ibid.
5. Jacques Lusseyran, *Blindness, A New Seeing of the World* (pamphlet), Myron Institute for Adult Education, New York 1973
6. Martin Buber, *Ten Rungs: Hasidic Sayings*, Schocken Books
7. Viktor Frankl, *Man's Search for Meaning – Experiences in a Concentration Camp*, Beacon Press 1959; originally *From Death Camp to Existentialism*, Hodder & Stoughton 1964

CHAPTER TEN

1. Krishnamurti, *Commentaries on Living*, Krishnamurti Writings Inc., 1956
2. Idries Shah, *The Wisdom of the Idiots*, Octagon Press 1969
3. Lao Tzu, *Tao Te Ching*, translated by D. C. Lau, Penguin Books 1963

4. Margaret Anderson, *The Unknowable Gurdjieff*, Routledge & Kegan Paul 1962
5. P. D. Ouspensky, *In Search of the Miraculous*, Harcourt, Brace & World 1949
6. A. J. Arberry, *Discourses of Rumi*, John Murray 1961
7. F. and A. Hyde-Chambers, *Tibetan Folk Tales*, Shambala 1981
8. Rabindranath Tagore, *Collected Poems and Plays*, Macmillan 1962
9. Lu Yu

CHAPTER ELEVEN

1. Farid Ud-din Attar, *The Conference of the Birds*, Routledge & Kegan Paul, Janus Press 1954
2. Idries Shah, *The Exploits of the Incomparable Mulla Nasrudin*, Octagon Press 1985
3. Irmis B. Popoff, *Gurdjieff*, Samuel Weiser 1969
4. J. Krishnamurti, *The Flight of the Eagle*, Harper & Row
5. Viktor Frankl, *Man's Search for Meaning – Experiences in a Concentration Camp*, Beacon Press 1959; originally *From Death Camp to Existentialism*, Hodder & Stoughton 1964
6. ibid.
7. Gurdjieff Pupils, *Views From the Real World*, Routledge & Kegan Paul 1976
8. Juan Mascaro, *The Upanishads*, Penguin
9. Viktor Frankl, *op cit*
10. ibid.
11. ibid.

CHAPTER TWELVE

1. Farid Ud-din Attar, *The Conference of the Birds*, Routledge & Kegan Paul, Janus Press 1954
2. C. S. Nott, *The Teaching of Gurdjieff – a Journal of a Pupil*, Routledge & Kegan Paul 1961
3. Shunryu Suzuki, *Zen Mind, Beginner's Mind*, John Weatherhill Inc. 1970
4. C. G. Jung, *Psychological Reflections*, Ark Paperbacks

5. C. S. Nott, op. cit.
6. Margaret Anderson, *The Unknowable Gurdjieff*, Routledge & Kegan Paul 1962
7. Shunryu Suzuki, op. cit.
8. Hasidic story
9. Rabbi Bunam of Pzhysha
10. Shunryu Suzuki, *op. cit.*
11. Henry Corbin, *The Man of Light in Iranian Sufism*, Shambala 1971
12. Martin Buber, *Ten Rungs: Hasidic Sayings*, Schocken Books
13. Simone Weil, *Reflections of the Love of God*

CHAPTER THIRTEEN

1. Shunryu Suzuki, *Zen Mind, Beginner's Mind*, John Weatherhill Inc. 1970
2. Chogyam Trungpa, *Meditation in Action*, Watkins Publishers 1969
3. Chogyam Trungpa, *Journey Without Goal*, Prajna Press
4. Idris Shah, *The Wisdom of the Idiots*, Octagon Press 1969
5. Chogyam Trunpa, *The Myth of Freedom and the Way of Meditation*, Shambala 1976
6. Lionel Blue, *A Backdoor to Heaven*, Darton, Longman & Todd 1979 and Fount Paperbacks 1985
7. *Ancient Book of Aphorisms*
8. Simone Weil, *Gateway to God*, Fount Paperbacks 1974
9. F. and A. Hyde-Chambers, *Tibetan Folk Tales*, Shambala 1981
10. Tsong Khapa

CHAPTER FOURTEEN

1. P. D. Ouspensky, *In Search of the Miraculous*, Harcourt, Brace & World 1949
2. Trevor Leggett, *Encounters in Yoga and Zen*, Routledge & Kegan Paul
3. Cecil Lewis, *A Way To Be*, Fount Paperbacks 1977, Fine Books Oriental 1984
4. Marcus Aurelius

5. Margaret Anderson, *The Unknowable Gurdjieff*, Routledge & Kegan Paul 1962
6. J. Krishnamurti, Brockwood Park Lecture, September 1981, Krishnamurti Foundation Trust 1984
7. Chogyam Trungpa, *The Myth of Freedom and the Way of Meditation*, Shambala 1976
8. The Ven. Ajahn Sumedho, *Now is the Knowing*, Funny Press, Bangkok
9. idem
10. Shunryu Suzuki, *Zen Mind, Beginner's Mind*, John Weatherhill Inc. 1970
11. Martin Buber, *The Way of Man*, Routledge & Kegan Paul
12. Leggett, op. cit.

CHAPTER FIFTEEN

1. Simone Weil, *Waiting on God*, Routledge & Kegan Paul 1951 and Fount Paperbacks 1959
2. ibid.
3. J. E. Brown, *The Sacred Pipe: Black Elk's Account*, Penguin
4. Thomas Merton, *Zen and the Birds of Appetite*, New Directions 1968
5. Cecil Lewis, *A Way To Be*, Fount Paperbacks 1977 and Fine Books Oriental 1984
6. Jean Vaysse, *Towards Awakening*, Routledge & Kegan Paul 1980
7. Gurdjieff Pupils, *Views from the Real World*, Routledge & Kegan Paul 1976
8. Chogyam Trungpa, *Journey Without Goal*, Prajna Press
9. Shunryu Suzuki, *Zen Mind, Beginner's Mind*, John Weatherhill Inc. 1970
10. René Zuber, *Who Are You, Monsieur Gurdjieff?*, Routledge & Kegan Paul 1980
11. Chogyam Trungpa, *The Myth of Freedom and the Way of Meditation*, Shambala
12. Janwillem van de Wetering, *The Empty Mirror*, Routledge & Kegan Paul 1973

CHAPTER SIXTEEN

1. Eugen Herrigel, *Zen and the Art of Archery*, Arkana 1953
2. Martin Buber, *Ten Rungs: Hasidic Sayings*, Schocken Books
3. J. Krishnamurti, *Commentaries on Living*, Krishnamurti Writings Inc. 1956
4. Hazkat Inayat Khan, *The Sufi Message*, Barrie & Jenkins, Rockliff 1962
5. Luis S. R. Vas, *The Mind of Krishnamurti*, Jaico Publishing House 1973
6. Shunryu Suzuki, *Zen Mind, Beginner's Mind*, John Weatherhill Inc. 1970

CHAPTER SEVENTEEN

1. Kahlil Gibran, *The Prophet*, Heinemann 1926
2. H. Polano, *The Talmud*, Frederick Warne
3. Martin Buber, *Between Man and Man*, Collins/Fount Paperbacks
4. Martin Buber, *Legends of the Baalshem*
5. Trevor Leggett, *Encounters in Yoga and Zen*, Routledge & Kegan Paul
6. C. G. Jung, *Psychological Reflections*, Ark Paperbacks
7. Chogyam Trungpa, *Journey Without Goal*, Prajna Press
8. c. G. Jung, ibid.
9. Gurdjieff Pupils, *Views from the Real World*, Routledge & Kegan Paul 1976

CHAPTER EIGHTEEN

1. Farid Ud-din Attar, *The Conference of the Birds*, Routledge & Kegan Paul, Janus Press 1954
2. John Redtail Freesoul, *Breath of the Invisible*, Quest Theological Publishing 1986
3. Zen saying
4. Hasidic story
5. Zen saying
6. Doug Boyd, *Rolling Thunder*, Delta Books
7. Marcel Griaule, *Conversations With Ogotemmêli*, Oxford University Press

8. C. G. Jung, *Psychological Reflections*, Ark Paperbacks
9. Brave Buffalo, Standing Rock
10. Black Elk
11. Marcel Griaule, idem
12. Doug Boyd, op. cit.
13. C. G. Jung, ibid.
14. Viktor Frankl, *Man's Search for Meaning – Experiences in a Concentration Camp*, Beacon Press 1959; originally *From Death Camp to Existentialism*, Hodder & Stoughton 1964
15. Eugen Herrigel, *The Method of Zen*, Routledge & Kegan Paul 1980
16. John G. Neihardt, *The Sacred Pipe: Black Elk Speaks*, William Morrow & Co. 1932
17. American Indian chant

CHAPTER NINETEEN

1. Eugen Herrigel, *Zen and the Art of Archery*, Arkana 1953
2. Carlos Castaneda, *Journey to Ixtlan*, Touchstone Books, Simon & Schuster 1972
3. Ram Dass, with Stephen Levine, *Grist for the Mill*, Oxford University Press
4. C. G. Jung, *Psychological Reflections*, Ark Paperbacks
5. Francesca Freemantle and Chogyam Trungpa, *The Tibetan Book of the Dead*, Shambala 1975
6. Rabindraneth Tagore, *Collected Stories and Poems*, Macmillan
7. H. Polano, *The Talmud*, Frederick Warne
8. G. I. Gurdjieff, *Life is Real Only Then, When "I Am"*, Routledge & Kegan Paul, Triangle Editions 1979

CHAPTER TWENTY

1. Trevor Leggett, *Encounters in Yoga and Zen*, Routledge & Kegan Paul
2. Jacob Needleman, *Lost Christianity*, Doubleday & Co. 1980
3. ibid.
4. ibid.
5. Andrew Harvey, *A Journey in Ladakh*, Jonathan Cape 1983 and Flamingo

6. Fritz Peters, *Boyhood with Gurdjieff*, Wildwood House and E. P. Dutton 1964
7. J. Krishnamurti, Brockwood Park Lecture, September 1981, Krishnamurti Foundation Trust 1984
8. Jean Vaysse, *Towards Awakening*, Routledge & Kegan Paul
9. O. M. Burke, *Among the Dervishes*, E. P. Dutton 1973
10. John Redtail Freesoul, *Breath of the Invisible*, Quest Publications 1986
11. Jalal Ud-din Rumi in Shamsi Tabriz, *Selected Odes from the Dirani*, Cambridge University Press 1898

Suggested Reading List

The Unknowable Gurdjieff, Margaret Anderson
Rolling Thunder, Doug Boyd
Between Man and Man, Martin Buber
Good and Evil, Martin Buber
I and Thou, Martin Buber
Ten Rungs, Martin Buber
Journey to Ixtlan, Carlos Castaneda
Mount Analogue, René Daumal
All and Everything – Beelzebub's Tales To His Grandson, G. I. Gurdjieff
Meetings with Remarkable Men, G. I. Gurdjieff
Views From Another World, Gurdjieff Pupils
Our Life With Mr Gurdjieff, Thomas and Olga de Hartmann
Zen in the Art of Archery, Eugen Herrigel
Autobiographical Writings, Hermann Hesse
Journey to the East, Hermann Hesse
Narciss and Goldmund, Hermann Hesse
Siddhartha, Hermann Hesse
The Glass Bead Game, Hermann Hesse
Memories, Dreams and Reflections, C. G. Jung
Modern Man in Search of a Soul, C. G. Jung
Commentaries on Living, J. Krishnamurti
Tao Te Ching, Lao Tzu
The Four Loves, C. S. Lewis
Letters to Malcolm – Chiefly on Prayer, C. S. Lewis
Out of the Silent Planet, C. S. Lewis
Perelandra, C. S. Lewis
Surprised by Joy, C. S. Lewis
That Hideous Strength, C. S. Lewis

Till We Have Faces, C. S. Lewis
The Mark, Maurice Nicoll
The New Man, Maurice Nicoll
A Journal of a Pupil – The Teaching of Gurdjieff, C. S. Nott
Journey Through This World, C. S. Nott
On Love, A. R. Orage
A New Model of the Universe, P. D. Ouspensky
In Search of the Miraculous, P. D. Ouspensky
The Psychology of Man's Possible Evolution, P. D. Ouspensky
Zen Mind, Beginner's Mind, Shunryu Suzuki
Hymn of the Universe, Pierre Teilhard de Chardin
Le Milieu Divin, Pierre Teilhard de Chardin
Cutting Through Spiritual Materialism, Chogyam Trungpa
Journey Without Goal, Chogyam Trungpa
Meditation in Action, Chogyam Trungpa
The Tibetan Book of the Dead, Chogyam Trungpa and Francesca Freemantle
The Conference of the Birds, Farid Ud-din Attar
The Secret of the Golden Flower, Richard Wilhelm

Acknowledgements for Extracts

The author is grateful for permission to use extracts from the following works, all of which are also credited in the Notes. In some cases it has not proved possible to obtain written clearance, but if later enquiries show that publication details need to be changed, the correction will be made in any reprint.

Anderson, Margaret, *The Unknowable Gurdjieff*, Routledge & Kegan Paul, 1962
Arberry, A. J., *The Discourses of Rumi*, John Murray (Publishers) Ltd, 1961
Attar, Farid Ud-din, *The Conference of the Birds*, Routledge & Kegan Paul, 1954
Brown, J. E., *The Sacred Pipe: Black Elk's Account*, Penguin Books Ltd; copyright University of Oklahoma Press Inc., USA
Boyd, Doug, *Rolling Thunder*, Dell Publishing, USA
Buber, Martin, *Ten Rungs: Hasidic Sayings*, Schocken Books, New York; copyright Estate of Martin Buber
The Way of Man, Routledge & Kegan Paul
Burke, O. M., *Among the Dervishes*, Octagon Press Ltd., 1973
Frankl, Viktor, *Man's Search For Meaning*, Hodder & Stoughton Ltd
Gurdjieff, G. I., *Meetings with Remarkable Men*, Routledge & Kegan Paul
Gurdjieff Pupils, *Views From The Real World*, Routledge & Kegan Paul
Harvey, Andrew, *A Journey in Ladakh*, Jonathan Cape Ltd, 1983
Herrigel, Eugen, *The Method of Zen*, Routledge & Kegan Paul
Hesse, Hermann, *Autobiographical Writings*, ed. Theodore Ziolkowski and translated by Denver Lindley, Jonathan Cape Ltd, 1973

Jung, C. G., *Psychological Reflections*, Routledge & Kegan Paul
Krishnamurti, J., Brockwood Park Lecture, September 1981, Krishnamurti Foundation Trust Ltd, Brockwood Park, Bramdean, Hants SO24 0LQ
Leggett, Trevor, *Encounters in Yoga and Zen*, Routledge & Kegan Paul
Needleman, Jacob, *Lost Christianity*, Doubleday, New York; copyright Harold Matson Co., Inc., USA
Nicoll, Maurice, *Psychological Commentaries on the Teaching of Gurdjieff and Ouspensky*, Shambala, Boston, USA
Nott, C. S., *The Teachings of Gurdjieff – A Journal of a Pupil*, Routledge & Kegan Paul, 1961
Orage, A. R., *On Love*, Janus Press, 1974
Ouspensky, P. D., *In Search of the Miraculous*, Harcourt Brace Jovanovich, Inc., USA
Peters, Fritz, *Boyhood with Gurdjieff*, E. P. Dutton, copyright Russell & Volkening, New York, 1964
Post, Laurens Van der, *Jung and the Story of Our Time*, The Hogarth Press, 1976
Suzuki, Shunryu, *Zen Mind, Beginner's Mind*, John Weatherhill Inc., Tokyo
Trungpa, Chogyam, *Cutting Through Spiritual Materialism*, Shambala, Boston, USA, 1973
Journey Without Goal, Prajna Press, Boston, USA
Weil, Simone, *Waiting on God*, Routledge & Kegan Paul
Wetering, Janwillem van de, *The Empty Mirror*, Routledge & Kegan Paul, 1973

Also available in Fount Paperbacks

BOOKS BY WILLIAM JOHNSTON

Silent Music

A brilliant synthesis which joins traditional religious insights with the discoveries of modern science to provide a complete picture of mysticism – its techniques and stages, its mental and physical aspects, its dangers, and its consequences.

The Inner Eye of Love

"This is a lucid comparison and exposition of eastern and western mysticism, from Zen to the Cloud of Unknowing, which can do nothing but good all round."

Gerald Priestland, The Universe

The Mirror Mind

"William Johnston continues his first-hand studies of Zen meditation and Christian prayer . . . At his disposal he has had a twofold large and demanding literature. His use of it can be startlingly luminous."

Bernard Lonegan

The Wounded Stag

This book examines the Old and New Testaments, the Christian mystical tradition, the Eucharist and mystical prayer, and explains how these can lead to the resolution of the conflict within men's hearts. A book with a message for today.